The Better Shot

Step-by-Step Shotgun Technique with Holland and Holland

HOLLAND & HOLLAND

Holland & Holland, established in 1835, is one of London's oldest gun and rifle makers, and has had a long-lasting reputation for the excellence of its work and its advice to shooters around the world.

The Holland & Holland 'Royal' gun, illustrated overleaf, has been a symbol of the quality of London gun making for over 100 years. The trade mark 'Royal' was granted in the United Kingdom in 1885 and preceded the opening of Mr Harris Holland's new factory in Kensal Green, London in 1898 – a factory which is still the heart of the company's gun making skills, and where every component of a gun or rifle is made, fitted, and finished.

The first Holland & Holland Shooting School was also opened in Kensal Green in the late 1880's. It moved to Wembley in 1913, and then to its present site in the Duck's Hill Road, Northwood, just sixteen miles from central London, in 1933.

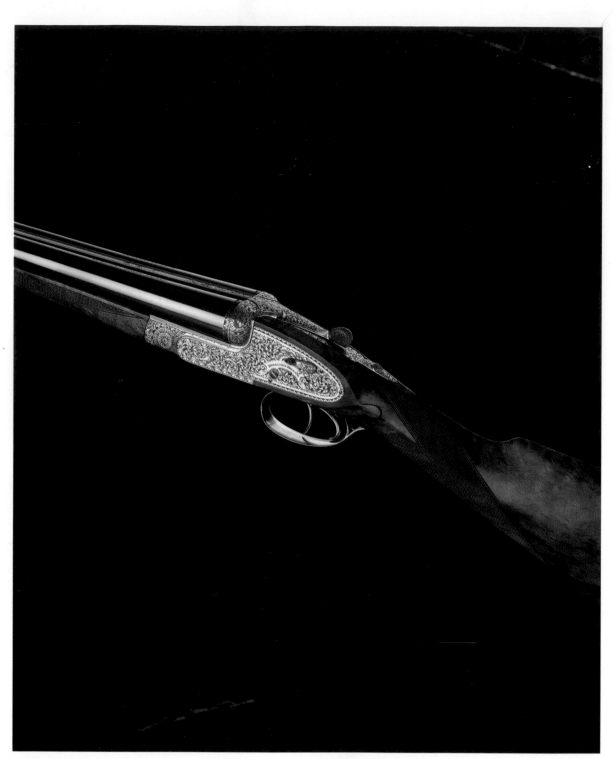

A fine example of present-day gun making. A 12-bore 'Royal' by Holland and Holland.

The Better Shot

Step-by-Step
Shotgun Technique
with Holland and Holland

Ken Davies

Quiller Press
London

DEDICATION

To the memory of Norman Clarke, whose boundless
enthusiasm and ability to coach the sport of shotgun
shooting inspired me over 25 years ago to follow
in his footsteps.

To Malcolm Lyell for his friendship and encouragement
over many years with HOLLAND & HOLLAND.

For the many thousands of shooters I have met over the
years who, often unwittingly, have helped me gain the
knowledge and experience which has made this book
possible, and to my wife who has painstakingly
'processed' my hand-written text.

*I am very glad that the book has been so successful and that
this second edition is now called for. I have taken the
opportunity to make some improvements. Good shooting!*

Ken Davies
Jan, 1996

First published 1992 by
Quiller Press Limited
46 Lillie Road
London SW6 1TN

Reprinted 1996

ISBN 1 870948 64 5

HOLLAND & HOLLAND is the trade mark of Holland and Holland Limited

Produced by Hugh Tempest-Radford *Book Producers* for Quiller Press
Typeset by Goodfellow & Egan Ltd, Cambridge
Printed in Italy by New Interlitho spa

Contents

		Page
Foreword by Jonathan Young		vii
Preface by Chris Cradock		ix
1	Starting Out	1
2	Method	5
3	Stance	13
4	Hands on the Gun	23
5	Gun Mounting	29
6	Gun Fit	41
7	Target 'Pick Up'	53
8	Safe Handling and Conduct in the Field	75
9	Ladies	107
10	Young Shooters	113
11	Working Two Guns with a Loader	117
12	Gun Care	129
13	Conclusion	131

PICTURE ACKNOWLEDGEMENTS

The publishers wish to thank the following for the illustrations supplied:
David Grewcock Copyright © 1992: Pages 85, 95, 96, 99, 102
Sotheby's: Page 128 (top)
Ben Hoskyns Copyright © 1992: Pages 9, 15, 16, 17, 56, 57, 66, 67, 68, 69, 70, 71, 72, 73, 92
Holland & Holland Copyright © 1992: Pages ii, vi, x, 4, 11, 12, 22, 28, 40, 50, 52, 74, 79, 106, 112, 116, 128 (bottom), 136

Foreword

by Jonathan Young
Editor of 'The Field'

I F a pheasant could think, it would head straight for the shot banging his stock into his cheek while trying to disentangle the overfed spaniel moored to a giant corkscrew. A wise bird would avoid the inert figure gazing silently up from under his cap. The first type of shot represents certain salvation; the second, the grim reaper in gumboots.

Most of us are neither. After years of trial and mostly error, we stumble across a shooting method that assures our share of the bag, leavened with occasional inspired patches, when we can kid ourselves that we really can shoot, and dark days which remind us that we cannot. Come the end of January, we have sorted out this season's problems and woe betide the next cock to come curling out from the hanger wood. Having reached this plateau of moderate consistency, the season ends. Nine months later, we start all over again.

Practice appears the remedy. It cannot be coincidental that the First X1 shots are also those who have the opportunity to do rather a lot of it. They will fire many thousands of cartridges a year; most of us will use under 500. The alternative is to shoot clay pigeons, thereby cramming into one day half a season's cartridge expenditure. (Those who proclaim airily that 'of course, they're not the real thing' are, invariably, those who cannot hit them.)

Yet practice is pointless, in fact ruinous, if all it does is instil deeper fundamental faults in our gun-handling acquired and embellished since the days we knocked down straggle-legged moorhens with our four-tens. We must practise the right things.

For 25 years, Ken Davies has been teaching the right way to shoot at the Holland & Holland shooting ground. A gameshooter himself, he understands that we do not want to be given the cheap confidence quickly acquired by simple clays floating over your head. Rather, we need to know, exactly how to cope with a right to left curling, tall crossing pheasant, or a quartering pair of grouse breaking out from the main pack with a 60mph wind up their tails.

Ken Davies always provides the solution, but not before he has ingrained accurate and consistent gun-mounting.

Different quarry species require different techniques and the main game species are dealt with separately in this book. Most useful, to my mind, is his advice on shooting birds well out in front. A pretty trick, it is, like so much good shooting, actually easier than the duffer's way. And who, after all, always wants to shoot like a duffer?

Despite our protestations that it's the day, not the shooting, that matters, no-one enjoys shooting badly. Apart from being a disappointment to all those who have worked so hard to present you with the birds, poor shooting is not fair to our quarry. A good shot kills, a bad shot misses altogether. It is the moderate shot who tinkers with his bird.

Close adherence to Ken Davies's philosophy will be enough, almost, to ensure clean kills on the most difficult of birds. The rest depends on practice, and the ability to convince the bank manager, and one's family, that it is essential to do more shooting.

Preface

by Chris Cradock

I WAS DELIGHTED to learn that Ken Davies, Chief Coach at Holland and Holland's long established Shooting School, has at last put pen to paper and produced this book. I have read and re-read the book and believe it to be a privilege to write this preface. I first met Ken Davies at a Game Fair back in the 1960's. Although we were working on different coaching stands I can remember Davies well. In those days Holland and Holland used a lovely horse-drawn carriage to collect clients for a shooting lesson from their stand in Gunmakers Row and ferry them to their coaching stand situated in the clay shooting section of the fair. It was obvious Ken had the young entry eating out of his hand—he still does. Since that time I have worked with him on coaching courses for BASC and others, also on *Shooting Times* shooting weekends and other teach ins. I have seen him coach and lecture many times. No matter who the client, Davies can quickly establish a rapport between a client and himself. He is one of the most accurate gun fitters for clay or game shooting I know. Regarding his book, Davies has distilled the essence of safe good shooting from a lifetime of practical coaching and shooting experience garnered from many parts of the world. His book covers the whole gamut of the art of safe, efficient handling of the shotgun. This in easy-to-understand English. Davies teaches safety at all times, he is a fine shot who can fully support his precepts with his superb shooting demonstrations.

The 150-odd photos are excellent and combine well with the text to provide the reader with the basic essentials required to enable any thinking shooter to eventually perform safely, efficiently and in close harmony with his gun. This book must surely become a classic, its sheer professionalism matching the high standards attained by the famous firm of London Gunmakers, Holland and Holland, of which Ken Davies is a Director. An ideal gift for any shooting person.

Chris Cradock.

The end of a lesson. The interior of the Holland & Holland Shooting School, Northwood.

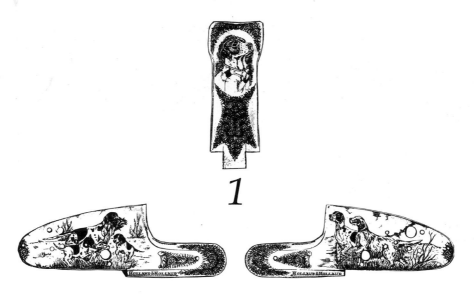

1

Starting Out

THROUGHOUT THIS book, with the exception of the section entitled 'Safe Handling and Conduct in the Field', my intention is not to make hard and fast rules which have to be followed in order to make things work, but to lay down basic guide-lines, from which through practice you can go on to build your own sound technique. Shooting a shotgun at moving targets—whether it be at live game or clay pigeons, where targets are presented through a wide variety of speeds, angles and distances throughout the effective range of the gun—can be likened in many ways to a game played with a small moving ball, e.g. cricket, tennis, squash, etc. It calls for the same co-ordination between hand and eye, the development of a similar sense of rhythm and timing, and the use of good footwork and body-swing to bring the whole thing together. To some people it seems to come easily, to a few—not at all; while for most of you who wish to do it well, it is a skill to be learned like any other. It requires time, patience, the discipline and wherewithal to practise, along with good constructive criticism and encouragement when needed.

Each person is different, so that what works for one does not necessarily work for the next, and it is this that makes coaching on a one to one basis generally so successful—and incidentally, so totally absorbing and rewarding for the coach. As with any sport, the basis lies in developing a good, sound technique, and then practising it until eventually everything can be done correctly, time after time, with little or no conscious effort. Only when you've reached this stage can you build up enough concentration on a target to hold it without distractions and make a successful shot.

Whichever shooting method, or combination of methods, you use—swing through, maintained lead and so on—there will always be room for experimentation and/or modification, before the best results are obtained. These modifications, along with variations in build, eye-sight, reaction time, general fitness, individual mannerisms, etc., will all go towards making one's own style as personal as one's finger-prints. Nevertheless, if improvement is to be maintained and on-going, then underlying each individual style there must remain a firm base: a solid base, well-learned and well-practised, so that under normal conditions, as a shot is taken, all the actions involved such as target pick-up, gun mounting, footwork, body swing and so on, can be made without thinking; a base to go back to and work up from again when things go wrong, as from time to time they inevitably will. To be successful, one overriding factor remains common to any method used, and that is keeping your concentration on the target as the shot is fired—in exactly the same way as you must 'keep your eye on the ball' as you hit or catch it well.

This build-up of concentration on the target cannot be over-emphasised, especially in situations where the gun muzzles quite clearly have to be ahead of the target in order to make a successful shot. With such shots there can be no getting away from the fact that for most people to deal with them effectively the gun muzzles must be ahead of the target as the shot is fired. Normally these are shots where there is an added time factor involved, e.g. long crossing targets or very high ones seen coming from a long way away; or perhaps a bird that appears to be going nowhere, flying into or across the wind – that slower ball presented after two or three fast deliveries that you react too quickly to and miss. One must of course be aware of the muzzles, and of the gap between them and the target, *but one's full hard focus must remain only on the target.* This is so important, as the movement of the gun, relative to the target, will only be maintained for as long as your concentration stays on that moving target. If you allow your concentration to leave the moving target (usually to look back at the end of the gun) then the gun will stop moving.

Building your own sight pictures

This gap between target and gun muzzles, that elusive factor referred to as 'lead', 'follow through' or 'forward allowance', still gives rise to much controversy and confusion. Each one of us is slightly different. We all see things in slightly different ways. Ask half a dozen good shots how they each deal successfully with the same sort of target and you are likely to get six different answers, all given in good faith, but each applying only to the individual in question. Each has, through practice, built up his or her own well-proven sight picture for that particular shot. Remember, as a basic guide line, that what works well for one does not necessarily work for the next. The shooter must build his own set of sight pictures for any given situation. Here perhaps is where

the competitive clay target shot has some advantage over the game shot, not only in knowing where each target is coming from, but also it's approximate line, speed and distance and where best to take it. As a result he can go through a simple system of checking stance, starting position, etc. and run over the shot in his mind before calling for each target. This 'check list' will often form part of what becomes an important preparatory ritual before each shot and is often coupled with a series of small actions such as the way the cartridges are lined up in the chambers, the way the gun is closed and the way the gaze is fixed on a particular point. The whole process will only take a second or two, but it becomes an important ploy (rather like a mini yoga exercise), used to clear the mind and focus attention on the task in hand. It helps build up and channel concentration in a situation where each shot is vital, where the fate of a single target can decide the result of a major competition.

Physical fitness naturally plays an important role in some forms of shooting, but the mental effort required to maintain high standards of performance during competition, or through a busy day in the game field, far outweighs the physical.

The game shot on the other hand has different problems to face: often he doesn't know when or from where the quarry may appear; nor does he know beforehand its line, speed or distance; he has to pick out specific targets, sometimes from a large number and has to identify legitimate targets before raising the gun; he doesn't always have the advantage of standing in reasonable comfort at a peg, but has to shoot while walking over rough ground, or from a crouched or seated position in a hide/blind. From a safety point of view, the game shot has to deal with the presence of, and distractions from, fellow guns, beaters, lookers-on, dogs, livestock, etc., all of whose safety must be taken into account.

This is not to say that the competition shot can ever ignore safety. In fact most serious competitors are exemplary in their safe gun handling—more so, dare I say, than many game shots. They quickly learn to load their guns only when on the shooting stations, to clear their guns before turning around and walking off the stations and to carry guns safely between shooting stations. Once on a shooting station, providing the organisers have done their work responsibly, there will be no-one, other than well-protected trap operators, and no live-stock in the shooting area, so that any target presented to the gun will be accepted, whether it has sky, trees or ground behind it. Many of us enjoy shooting at both game and clay targets and learn to behave correctly in either situation, but when the roles are reversed for the first time, both the game shot and the clay target shot can run into trouble without realising it, unless specifically directed otherwise beforehand: the game shot perhaps through loading the gun as he walks to a competition stand, instead of only when on the stand itself; by turning around and walking off the stand before opening and clearing the gun—the fact that both shots may have been fired is of no consequence; by walking between stations with an uncovered, closed gun; the clay shot, unless given prior guidance, by wanting to take every bird offered without due regard to range, resulting in some shots being

An understanding of the relationship between your gun muzzles and the target is essential for each shot. Ken Davies using cartridges to demonstrate the relationship.

taken at birds the experienced game shot would consider too close, too distant or too low to be sporting; or perhaps by shooting into backgrounds the game shot, for the sake of safety, would automatically avoid.

Norman Clarke, guide and inspiration to the author, waiting to shoot.

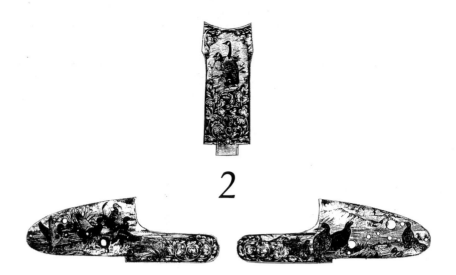

2

Method

In SHOTGUN shooting as in many sports a number of different methods have evolved, some seemingly more successful than others, and some having specialist application in particular disciplines. All have their following and many experienced shooters will use a combination of two or more techniques, often without even realising it.

The Churchill influence

Contrary to popular belief, the basic method taught at The Holland & Holland Shooting School in Northwood has never been 'pure Churchill'. It was Norman Clarke, who spent some 34 years with Churchill, who brought the method to the school at Northwood, when he was employed by Holland & Holland shortly after Churchill's death in 1958. When I joined the company in the mid 1960s, Norman was already teaching his own modified and adapted 'Churchill method', which has itself undergone changes since his own untimely death in 1970.

The method now taught retains many important 'Churchill' elements such as: a reasonably square, narrow stance so that body weight can be shifted easily over either foot; the same basic starting or 'ready' position; emphasis on the front hand in mounting and guiding the gun; similar footwork and bodyswing; and, perhaps above all else, the importance of

keeping absolute concentration on the target and not on the gun muzzles.

Two points in Churchill's teaching have always caused dispute, perhaps because they have been badly described or poorly interpreted in the past: firstly, that of always shooting at the target, i.e. with no conscious 'lead'; and secondly, letting off the gun as soon as it touches the shoulder. Norman Clarke did not really agree with either of these two points and never taught them in their strictest sense.

Seeing a lead

On the first point, that of always shooting at the target, emphasis was always, and is still, laid upon keeping absolute concentration on the target throughout the shot without ever looking back at the gun. Applying this principle, the feeling for many shooters, especially when dealing with relatively close, fast targets, would always be one of shooting right at the target with no conscious 'forward allowance'; while for others, even these 'instinctive' shots, especially those quartering or crossing from left to right (for right-handed shooters), would require some conscious 'allowance', a definite gap between target and muzzles, in order to connect. Here, perhaps, is where the controversy arises. What works well for one person does not necessarily work for the next. Some people need to see a conscious

A fairly square narrow stance (above left) to enable the shooter to move body weight easily from one foot to the other depending upon where the shot is to be taken, while keeping the same relationship between gun-stock, cheek and shoulder as when the gun is mounted straight ahead.

As illustrated here (above and left) with body weight well forward for a bolting rabbit shot, or coming onto the back foot for a high shot overhead.

On opposite page

A starting or 'ready' position with the heel of the gun-stock tucked up under the armpit to discourage the rear hand from lifting . . .

. . . and encourage the front hand to push the gun muzzles out towards the target.

. . . so that the gun is brought up into the sight-line with little or no head movement down to meet the stock, and the shoulder moving forward behind the stock to lock it firmly into place.

Picking up the target's line with the gun muzzles to judge line and speed correctly.

'lead' on certain shots, while others will apparently be able to shoot right at the target. This can only be learned by each individual executing the same shot successfully a number of times, in order to build and instil in the mind their own sight pictures, which, with practice, can be instantly recalled when the target is next presented. For anyone to be conscious of any sort of gap or 'lead' between target and gun as a shot is fired they must naturally be aware of the gun muzzles. The 'secret' here is never to let your eyes focus on the muzzles, but to keep full hard focus on the target at all times. It is this, and only this, that keeps the gun moving as the shot is fired. As a further complication, many beginners need to be quite conscious of giving certain targets a great deal of 'forward allowance' during their early lessons, while they are having to think hard about technique; but as their actions become more natural and less thought about through practice, more and more

concentration can be transferred to the target and the apparent 'lead' needed to break a target can decrease markedly.

To re-cap, each person must build his own sight pictures, and above all else keep his concentration on the target as the shot is fired.

Shooting as the gun comes up

I now turn to the second point, that of letting off the gun as soon as the stock touches the shoulder. Interpreted literally, this action never works well as an all-round technique, and can only result in the gun frequently being fired before the stock is fully mounted. What I think Churchill was trying to get away from was the other extreme, that of mounting the gun to the shoulder, often through using the rear hand, very early on in the shot and then spending a comparatively long time chasing after the target with a fully-mounted gun before firing the shot. This again can never work well as an all-round technique as, once the stock is mounted, it becomes difficult to move freely especially when dealing with crossing shots. Once

Walking Up—Pheasant going away.

1 *As spaniel flushes pheasant, the first action is that of bringing the gun stock up under the arm into the ready position.*

2 *As pheasant beings to fly away, gun has narrowed his stance and is beginning to pick up bird's line from below as the leading hand starts to mount the gun; body weight is moving forward towards bird.*

3 *Gun mount completed just before shot is fired; stock is well up into cheek, front arm well extended, body weight nicely forward.*

There is always more time than one thinks to make a shot; targets flying away usually tend to make one hurry causing bad gun mounting. Any time lost in bringing the gun to the 'ready position' is easily made up for in the speed and accuracy of the controlled gun mount.

the gun is in the shoulder, tension against expected recoil sets in. (Do not let this last statement take away the value of letting a beginner start shooting at basic targets with a pre-mounted gun, as this can prove invaluable in learning the correct shooting position at cheek and shoulder, correct target pick-up, etc. However, good gun mounting is such an important part of each shot, the beginner should try starting from the gun down, or 'ready' position as soon as possible.)

The stock then should not be fully mounted too soon, which results in a long swing, nor too late, with the shot sometimes fired before the gun is fully up. Ideally the gun should be moving freely along the target's line as it is being mounted, with the front hand largely controlling both actions. The stock becomes fully mounted at the cheek and shoulder just before the target is caught, or passed, so that there is a moment when everything comes firmly together before the shot is fired.

The Holland and Holland method

This modified Churchill/Clarke style presently taught at Northwood is now widely regarded as the most natural and successful way for the majority of shooters to deal with the wide variety of targets presented by game birds and sporting clay pigeons. It is well established and accepted world-wide and could now be referred to as the Holland & Holland method.

Briefly, this method employs a fairly square narrow stance to enable the shooter to move body weight easily from one foot to the other, depending upon where the shot is to be taken. A starting or 'ready' position with the heel of the gun stock tucked up under the armpit to discourage the rear hand from lifting, and encourage the front hand to push the gun muzzles out towards the target in order to mount the gun. This is the mount where the front hand pushes the gun out towards the target, bringing the gun up into your sight-line and the comb of the stock up into the cheek, with little or no head movement down to meet the stock. The shoulder moves in behind the butt of the stock, as opposed to the stock being pulled back against the shoulder. When mounted correctly in this way, the gun should be fitted to throw its shot charge a little high.

When picking up the target's line with the gun muzzles (and therefore the front hand), at a point just sufficiently far behind the target to judge its line, speed and distance correctly, you should let everything come firmly together (i.e. completing the gun mount) a moment before the muzzles catch up with (as in low straight going away or low straight on-coming targets) or overtake the target and the shot is fired.

The emphasis is on building up and maintaining concentration on the target throughout the shot.

Up to now I have tried to use the terms 'front' and 'rear' as opposed to 'left' and 'right'. However, for the sake of clarity in parts of the following text, I will be talking about shooting from the right shoulder. For those of you shooting from the left shoulder, my apologies, but you should not find it difficult to reverse the instructions where necessary.

A superb example of the art of gun making is the 20-bore Holland & Holland Quail gun No. 40595, built in 1986. The various coloured gold inlays portray five of the thirty-eight species of quail in the world, inlaid by the world renowned Ken Hunt. The call of the quail is inlaid in silver and gold musical notes on the barrels and the gun was supplied in a Harewood case with marquetry inlay depicting Bobwhite and California Quail, the case lining in leather.

Trade samples of Damascus Tubes. The beauty of Damascus gun barrels is self-evident and visually illustrates a depth of skill and workmanship seldom appreciated by the casual observer. The fourth tube from the top clearly shows the name Joseph in pattern of the twist. Patterns vary by using different forms of twisted rods of iron and steel and there is virtually no limit to the variation of patterns that can be obtained by the natural welding process.

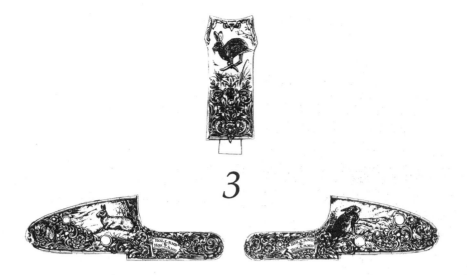

3

Stance

THERE IS A great deal of truth in the saying 'a good shot starts from your feet', and this of course applies to many sports other than shotgun shooting. A good stance should leave your body relaxed and comfortable, and help present the correct 'shoulder pocket' for the butt of the gun-stock. It must provide a balanced working base over which your body weight can be moved easily forwards or backwards, or

A good stance should leave your body relaxed and comfortable, and help present the correct 'shoulder-pocket' for the butt of the gun-stock. Compare this with . . .

pivoted freely over either foot as a turn is made, depending on where the shot is to be taken. It should enable you to keep the same relationship between gun-stock, cheek and shoulder when the gun is

A typical 'rifleman's' stance, adopted by many beginners who have perhaps used an air-rifle or .22 rimfire weapon. The stance is too wide and too sideways on to the front throwing back the right shoulder. In consequence the right hand has had to lift the gun stock up and back into the cheek and shoulder. The stock is not in fact on the shoulder but out on the top of the biceps and the body weight is back on the heels—no way to take recoil, reach for the ice-pack!

This photograph taken from below clearly shows the stock well into the correct 'shoulder pocket', along with a good view of the rear hand grip showing good clearance between trigger-guard and second-finger.

To take up the basic position, imagine yourself standing on a large clock face. Using your feet as the hands of the clock, point your left toes towards the figure twelve and your right toes towards the two, keeping your heels about 6" apart. Do not be afraid to experiment a little with this basic stance, as depending on your individual build, you may well find that by pointing your left foot more towards one on the clock rather than twelve, and the right toes more towards three than two, that you make yourself a better base for all round movement and ease of gun mounting.

Footwork and body swing

This stance then is an 'ideal' which comes into its own when standing waiting for driven game. It allows you to move your body weight well forward for shots taken out in front, to be evenly balanced over both feet as targets get closer and higher and, when necessary, to bring your weight onto the back foot to help deal with really high overhead shots. With crossing and quartering birds you will find that, with a little practice, you can turn easily to both sides by pivoting over either foot (left to turn left, right to turn right). When shooting from the right shoulder, the turn to the left side is normally a very natural movement, while the turn to the right is a more awkward movement against the body. Both turns, but especially the turn to the right, can be helped by pushing your body around with the opposite toes, so that by the time the shot is taken, most of your weight is firmly over the foot from which you are shooting. This basic stance will serve the sporting clay shot as well as the game shot, the only variation being that when dealing with crossing shots, in particular those going from left to right, it is helpful to take up the stance facing the area in which you expect to break the target (knowing of course already the line along which the targets will be thrown). Then, by turning your body back towards the point where you first expect to pick up the target with the gun muzzles, you can 'unwind' and turn easily back through the 'killing area' as the shot is made. The same advice does not usually work so well with targets

mounted correctly wherever the shot is taken, and at the same time allow you to keep the gun moving freely, as and after the shot is fired, while still keeping the gun muzzles squarely on the target's line. To these ends keep your stance narrow rather than wide, your feet about shoulder width apart, as it is much easier to shift your weight from one foot to the other over a close stance than a wide one. Widening the stance an inch or two though, can help when dealing with low going away, low oncoming and low crossing shots, where it is necessary to keep plenty of weight forward towards the target. When dealing with high targets your feet are best kept close together, heels no more than about 6" apart, so that your weight can be moved onto the back foot if necessary for really high oncomers, and where the pivoting turns on high quartering and crossing shots call for an altogether more upright stance.

Crossing Partridge—from left to right.
1 *Gun sees or hears birds approaching and comes into 'ready position'; good stance, stock up under arm, muzzles at safe height just above hedgerow where he first expects to pick up target.*

2 *Front arm being used to pick up bird's flight line with gun muzzles and to begin gun mount. This is the unnatural swing from the right shoulder, so requires more effort from body and feet to keep gun moving smoothly through bird.*

3 *Gun mount completed just before bird is overtaken; body turning well to face bird squarely throughout the shot, feet being used well as turn is made. Weight pivoting over right foot, left foot helping to push the body around.*

4 *Gun overtakes bird as shot is taken, more consciously so on this side (the unnatural swing for the right-handed shooter), body still turning well to face bird squarely (right shoulder kept well up). Footwork and body swing continue after shot is taken to give good follow through.*

Crossing partridge from right to left.
1 *Gun sees or hears birds approaching and comes into 'ready position'; good stance, stock up under arm, muzzles at safe height just above hedgerow where he first expects to pick up target.*

3 *Front arm extended as gun mount is completed just before muzzles catch up with bird. Turn continues to face bird as more body weight pivots over left foot.*

crossing from right to left. In this case, if you stand facing the 'killing area', it can be difficult to get the muzzles back to the correct pick-up point, as you are having to force the gun, against your body, into a strained and uncomfortable posture, or wait with the muzzles so far round to the left that the result is an intercepting approach. This often causes a miss, or a late shot, when you have to wait for the target

2 *Front arm being used to both pick up bird's flight line and begin gun mount. This is the natural swing when shooting from the right shoulder; body is beginning to turn slowly to face the bird but not much footwork yet.*

4 *Muzzles smoothly overtake bird as shot is fired; footwork and body swing continue for a moment after firing to give good follow through.*

to pass the gun muzzles before being able to get onto its line correctly. Better on this side, to stand facing the point where you first expect to pick up the target with the gun, and let your natural swing from right to left take over. Do not be afraid to experiment a little. Each hit or miss should teach you something, and help you find your optimum starting point for any given situation.

A balanced base over which your body weight can be moved easily forwards or backwards, or pivoted freely over either foot as a turn is made. Gun is in the 'ready' position.

Body weight moving forward over front foot as gun is mounted to take low shot in front.

Even more weight forward for shot on ground at 'bolting rabbit'.

Note the gun change. Here the weight is still on the front foot, but less so for a medium oncoming shot taken out in front.

Weight beginning to more back and is now evenly balanced over both feet for a reasonably high oncoming target or perhaps the second shot at an approaching pair.

'Le coup de roi', body weight now well back from the waist, firmly over the back foot for a really high overhead target.

▲ ▲

Turning for a crossing target to the left, viewed from behind and above. The body is turned to face square on to the target, with weight over the left foot and going towards the target. The right toes beginning to help push the body around, left shoulder kept well up. The view from above clearly shows how the body is turned to face square on to the target.

Similar views for a higher target crossing to the left. Here the body is held more upright though weight is still over the left foot, and has again been turned to face the target squarely. The left shoulder is kept well up.

▼ ▼

▲

Turning for target crossing to the right, viewed from behind and above. The body is turned squarely to face the target as the shot is fired. With this, the unnatural swing for right handers a little more help from the opposite foot is called for to help push the body around. The weight is well forward over the right foot, going towards the target, this time the right shoulder is kept up well to stay on target line.

▲

Similar views for a higher crossing target to the right. More upright stance, but still with good pivoting turn to face target squarely. Good view of stock in shoulder pocket.

▼

▼

◄

Here the stance has been changed to take an expected target crossing to the right. Taking up the stance initially facing the area where the shot is expected to be taken, turning the body, and of course the gun muzzles back towards the trap and unwinding as the target appears. This works much better on the right turn than the left turn, when shooting from the right shoulder.

Leaning towards crossing targets, instead of turning to face them when making a shot inevitably leads to the familiar 'rainbowing', or dropped shoulder action. Often caused by keeping

too much weight over the heels of both feet, the result can only be a shot off the line of the target, usually below.

◄

Widening the stance an inch or two though can help when dealing with low shots where it is necessary to keep plenty of weight forward towards the target, as here when setting up for a 'bolting rabbit' shot. Good starting position, with stock well up under the arm and muzzles down just below line of expected target.

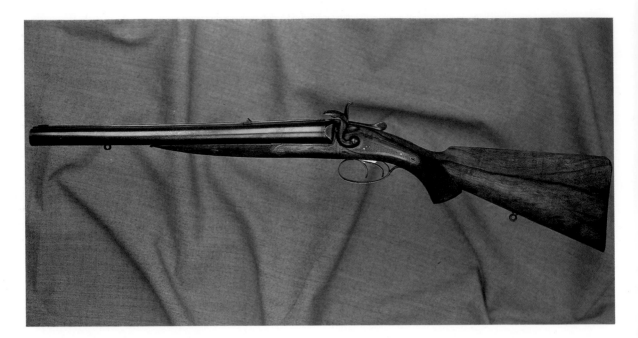

One of a pair of very rare 10-bore Holland & Holland black powder, Howdah shot or ball carbines. The sighted Damascus barrels are 15" in length. The back action hammer mechanism is unique being of dual system pin fire and percussion. Gun No. 5032 made for Mr Newman in 1878. Due to the dual system it has an unusual feature for the pin fire gun. It is fitted with an extractor which lifts out either the pin fire or the centre fire case.

A very rare 12-bore Holland & Holland hammer gun No. 4678. The mechanism is built on Perke's self-cocking system wherein the hammers are cocked mechanically on opening. Made in 1877. When the gun is opened a cocking arm, connected to the base of the first lump, is raised and comes into contact with the hammers through the top of the action, forcing both the hammers to the cocked position. Perke's Patent No. 129, dated 1876.

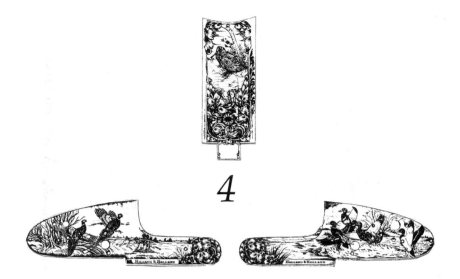

4

Hands on the Gun

ANY NEWCOMERS to shotgun shooting, both young and old, will already have done some work with a rifle, even if only with an air or .22 rim-fire weapon. Although this can be an excellent introduction to shooting sports in general, it can also lead to the development of a number of habits which unless corrected early on will prove detrimental to their shotgun work. This is not to say that an individual cannot perform well with both shotgun and rifle, but the two techniques should be treated separately and not mixed.

The leading hand (left hand/front hand)
Unlike rifle shooting where, generally speaking, carefully aimed shots are taken at stationary targets and where the leading hand is often used purely as a rest to support the weapon from below, in shotgun work this is the all-important hand. It is the hand which guides the gun muzzles, the muzzles becoming an extension of this hand, so that where the leading hand points the shot will go. It is also the hand which should be used to do most of the gun mounting.

The leading (front) hand, the hand which guides the muzzles. The muzzles should become an extension of this hand so that where it points the shot will go. Note continuing extension of left arm throughout the mounting action.
These three photographs show the front arm pushing out well.

Leading hand grips the barrels of the side-by-side gun, out towards the end of the wedge fore-end. Thumb and fingers are each side of the barrels.

Leading hand grip, viewed from above shows thumb and fingers clear of top of barrels and top-rib.

Leading hand grip, acceptable variation with first finger extended below barrels.

Leading hand grip on under-and-over gun where larger fore-end is designed to be held.

Leading hand grip on under-and-over gun, viewed from other side, showing first finger extended along fore-end wood. A variation favoured by some as an aid to pointing.

Grip. On the standard side-by-side game gun, furnished with a traditional wedge or splinter-style fore-end and having the correct length of stock, the leading hand should hold the gun towards the end of the fore-end wood, gripping the barrels, not the wood. The wedge fore-end is not designed to be held. The thumb is placed to lie pointing forwards along the side of the left barrel, with the hand cupped so that the pads of the fingers lie along the side of the right barrel. The palm of the hand should remain hollow so that the grip is firm yet light. In this position the user will have a clear view over the barrels and top-rib when the gun is correctly mounted. The thumb and fingers should not be allowed to encroach over the top of the barrels or top-rib as this can cause the gun to become canted when mounted. It can also cause shots to go low when the stock is mounted correctly, as the user is having to view targets over his thumb or fingers. The longer, bulkier beaver-tail fore-end found on some side-by-side guns—often those made for the American sportsman—may well detract a little from the classic lines of the gun, but it is much more practical to hold and does away with the need for the use of a handguard which, if used carelessly, can cause damage to both barrels and traditional fore-end. If the gun gets uncomfortably hot in use, or a better grip is needed on the barrels, wear a well-fitting, thin leather glove on the front hand.

On under-and-over shotguns,

Rear hand grip with first finger extended to lie along trigger-guard below front trigger

Rear hand, pad of first finger on front trigger, good gap between rear of trigger-guard and base of second finger to avoid bruising. Thumb well clear of safety-catch and top-lever.

Rear hand grip viewed from other side showing good gap between trigger-guard and base of second finger, thumb curled over grip (hand) of stock.

Even with this single-trigger the first finger should not go too far around it, just down to the crease of the first-joint to allow easy trigger release between shots and so that the second-finger stays clear of the trigger guard.

increasingly used in the game field these days, the much bigger fore-end, made in a variety of shapes, is of course designed to be held. The grip is as previously described except that it is taken up on the wood and the palm is filled more than it would be by the barrels of the side-by-side gun. The whole configuration of the under-and-over barrels, plus the much deeper fore-end section, make it virtually impossible for thumb or fingers to creep over the top barrel or rib. With either gun an acceptable variation to this grip is with the first finger

extended underneath the barrels or fore-end of a side-by-side or alongside the fore-end of an under-and-over, if it is felt that this is an aid to pointing and guiding the gun.

The right hand/rear hand
Most side-by-side game guns are built with two triggers and a straight-hand grip to the stock. To take up the correct position

Definitely not the place for your thumb when pulling the trigger as the recoil of the shot will drive the end of the top-lever straight into the top of your thumb.

Both hands in good position on the gun. For the observant pictures 8 through 14 show the slightly unusual combination of a side-by-side gun with single-trigger and an under-and-over gun with double triggers.

for the rear hand on such a stock, place the palm of the hand on the outside of the grip so that the grip lies diagonally across the palm from the base of the first finger to the heel of the hand. Curl all four fingers around the grip so that the second joint of the first finger just touches the back of the trigger-guard and wrap the thumb over the top of the grip behind and well clear of the safety-catch. Now, without moving the hand forward, extend the first finger so that it lies along the trigger-guard just below the triggers. From this position if the finger is brought onto the front trigger, the trigger should lie across the base of the finger pad just in front of the first joint and the finger can now be moved easily from front to back trigger without having to slide the whole hand back along the stock to do so. Having moved the first finger onto the trigger-guard, without sliding the hand forward, there should now be ample clearance between the back of the trigger-guard and the base of the second finger, an area often bruised by recoil, particularly when using a lightweight game gun, when the gun is held incorrectly. If the first finger is wrapped too far around the front trigger, a habit often carried over from rifle shooting where such a grip is necessary in order to

carefully squeeze off a shot without disturbing the aim, then the base of the second finger is pulled up against the back of the trigger-guard, resulting in a painful blow to the finger each time a shot is fired. With the first finger wrapped too far around the front trigger, it also becomes much more difficult to move it freely between the two triggers. As a result the whole hand has to be moved back in order to use the rear trigger, so disturbing the overall hold on the gun.

For anyone with small hands or very short fingers, sometimes the only cure for bruising the base of the second finger may be a change from double triggers to single trigger.

Some of you with very large hands may also find bruising occurring on the second finger. This is usually because the comb of the stock is butting up too hard against the ball of your thumb, pushing the whole hand forward behind the trigger-guard. Cutting back the comb of the stock by ½ an inch or so will have the effect of lengthening the grip of the stock, allowing the whole hand to be moved slightly rearwards to give the necessary clearance between second finger and trigger-guard.

Top: *One of a pair of very rare 10-bore Holland & Holland black powder, Howdah shot or ball carbines. The sighted Damascus barrels are 15" in length. The back action hammer mechanism is unique being of dual system pin fire and percussion. Gun No. 5032 made for Mr Newman in 1878. Due to the dual system it has an unusual feature for the pin fire gun. It is fitted with an extractor which lifts out either the pin fire or the centre fire case.*

Bottom: *A very rare 12-bore Holland & Holland hammer gun No. 4678, made in 1877. The mechanism is built on Perke's self-cocking system wherein the hammers are cocked mechanically on opening. When the gun is opened a cocking arm, connected to the base of the first lump, is raised and comes into contact with the hammers through the top of the action, forcing both the hammers to the cocked position. Perke's Patent No. 1229, dated 1876.*

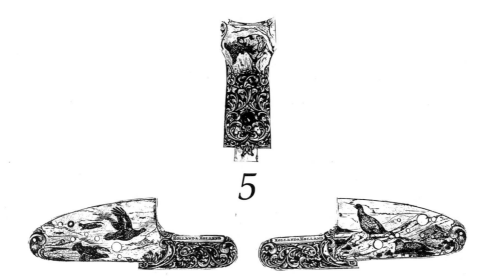

5

Gun Mounting

Put simply, a well-fitted gun is one which, when mounted correctly, points where you look. Small mistakes made in mounting the stock to your cheek and shoulder will quickly become bigger ones at 20, 30 and 40 yards. No matter how much trouble you take to ensure that your gun fits well, consistently good results can only come through good consistent gun mounting.

Once learned, good gun mounting with a well-fitted gun is basically a very easy, economical action, though the number of variations on the theme which people come up with seems endless and never ceases to amaze.

Bad mounting

Far and away the most common mistake made when bringing up the gun to the shooting position is that of lifting the stock with the right hand; it is, after all, the most natural thing to do, as most people shooting from the right shoulder will be right-handed. The right hand (arm) then is the stronger of the two—especially for those who perhaps play racquet sports or fly-fish— and, unless controlled, will tend to dominate the mounting action. The action of lifting with the right hand can cause a number of errors:

Most commonly, the stock comes up too high both on the shoulder and at the cheek, with an opposite downward see-sawing action at the muzzles, resulting in the shot going below the target and sometimes to its left-hand side. The high mount also often bruises both the cheek and the shoulder. The cheek because the comb of the stock is forced up too high underneath the angle of the cheek bone, instead of firmly against the fleshy pad of the cheek where your teeth come together. In extreme cases the stock may be brought up so high that it lies against the outside of the cheek bone, with very painful results. With the stock in this position, the leading eye will no longer be directly over the top-rib of the gun, and the shot will tend to go to the left of, as well as below, the target. Bruising will also occur on the shoulder or collar-bone as when the stock is brought up too high, the heel will be above the top of the shoulder, with only the pointed toe of the stock in contact with the shoulder. Remember those physics lessons? Pressure = Force over Area! Felt recoil is then transferred painfully through a small, sometimes sharp area of the butt, instead of being evenly dispersed over the relatively flat surface area of the whole butt, when the gun is correctly mounted.

Oddly enough, lifting with the right hand can also cause shots to go high. Usually this occurs when using too long a stock or when wearing extra layers of clothing against the weather. The lifting action of the right hand now causes the heel of the stock to catch and stick low in

Once learned, good gun mounting with a well fitted gun is basically a very easy, economical action . . .

Above: Ready/starting position.

Halfway stage

Completed mount.

... though the number of variations which people come up with never ceases to amaze. Most commonly, the stock comes up too high both on the shoulder and at the cheek, with an opposite downward action at the muzzles, resulting in the shot going below the target.

Viewed from the front, resulting in the shot going low.

In extreme cases, it may be brought up so high that it lies against the outside of the cheek-bone, with only the pointed toe of the stock in contact with the shoulder.

Lifting with the right (rear) hand can also cause shots to go high, usually when the heel of the stock catches and sticks low in the shoulder. This can be

aggravated by using too long a stock or putting on extra clothing against the wet or cold.
Above: Too low in the shoulder.

Viewed from the front, the shot must go high.

the shoulder and, in consequence, unless the head is ducked down unnaturally to compensate, the comb of the stock does not contact the cheek but lies across the lower jaw-bone. Inevitably the shot will go high and bruising can occur on the shoulder with felt recoil now passing only through the small area of the heel instead of the whole surface area of the butt, or more usually on the lower jaw where the comb of the stock touches the bone. A useful point to remember here is that when wearing extra clothing against the cold, you can effectively reduce the apparent stock length by slightly shortening your left-hand grip on the barrels or fore-end, and this will have the desired effect.

Apart from causing problems at both cheek and shoulder, the right-hand lift can cause a loss of balance, putting the body weight too far back on the heels instead of over the balls of the feet. If this does not affect the first shot, it certainly will the second, as the recoil of the first shot cannot be taken well if the body weight is already back on the heels before the first shot is taken. This, by the way, should not be confused with the deliberate transfer of weight over the back foot (not the heel) recommended when taking high oncoming birds overhead.

The other main cause of bad gun mounting is head movement down to meet the stock during the mounting action. Your head must be kept still and the gun brought

Raising the rear elbow too high during the mount changes the shape of the shoulder pocket and cants the gun to the left.

Fingers of the front hand gripping over top of barrel exerting twisting action of gun during mount. Gun becomes canted to right.

up into your sight-line—never try to drop your sight-line down to the gun. If your head moves, then your whole body should go with it, as in going away or passing shots. Your head must not move independently from your body. For most driven game shooters this simply involves standing up reasonably straight, keeping your head up in a natural position, and bringing the gun up into your sight-line when a target appears. Most competition shooters tend to adopt a slightly more aggressive stance before calling for a target,

and this often means that the head is lowered slightly, or turned a little to the right before the gun is mounted. This is fine, providing that the same posture is adopted each time.

What we are looking for all the while is consistent positioning of the gun stock into the shoulder pocket and cheek. Moving your head down, or tilting it over to meet the stock during the actual gun mount, can only prevent the gun from coming up correctly. It will cause shots to go high, and left and, depending on the degree of head

Thumb lying over top-rib means target has to be viewed over thumb. Shots will go low as a result.

Shortening the grip on the front hand slightly can effectively reduce the apparent stock length (good mount).

movement made during the mount, can cause bruising on the shoulder, top of the arm, jaw-bone or cheek-bone.

With many beginners both these faults are often caused through hurrying to bring up the gun, the feeling being that there are too many actions to make in the time available. A little disciplined practice though, particularly once you begin doing things correctly and in the right sequence, will soon demonstrate that there is always more time than you think. Bad habits such as these, if left unchecked and perhaps practised without guidance for a year or two, will become so ingrained that they become very difficult to correct. If you wear

ear-muffs while shooting, wear them properly adjusted for height with the band fitting snugly over your head, when you practise your gun mounting. If, as you mount the gun, the comb or heel of the stock hits the lower edge of the muff this is a good indication that you are either lifting the stock up too high with your right hand, or ducking your head down too low—probably the former.

The right way
Having tackled two of the main causes of bad gun mounting, I want to dwell on how things are done the right way. Contrary to popular belief, mounting a shotgun well does not entail putting the butt of the gun stock to your shoulder! A good gun mount comes partly from doing quite the

Keep your head still and bring the gun up into your sight-line.

Here the head has been dropped down during the mounting action preventing the stock from coming up fully. This may well cause the shot to go high and left, even if you get away with it on the first shot the stock will move markedly with the recoil and make recovery for a second shot very difficult.

opposite—putting your shoulder onto the butt of the gun-stock. So let me now try to explain how to set about doing this. The essence of a good gun mount is, in fact, the action of pushing or pointing the gun away from your body, and of course towards the target, with your left (front) hand. Think that over for a moment, and let it sink in. The left hand, the one that guides your gun muzzles, is the really important one in this game. The muzzles should become an extension of your left arm so that where your left hand goes, your shot will follow. As far as possible the left hand and arm should do the bulk of the work in mounting the gun, and in getting the muzzles of the gun onto the target's line.

Time for a quick re-cap: to mount the gun well you need to keep your head still, and in as natural a position as possible. You will keep your head still (and this is perhaps the most important point of all) by building up and keeping your concentration on the target as the shot is fired; you must discourage the right hand from lifting up the stock, and encourage the left hand to push the gun away from your body, towards the target; and finish the shot with the comb of the stock bedded firmly against the fleshy pad of your cheek and the shoulder pocket bedded firmly in behind the butt of the stock. In this position the comb of the stock should not press hard against your lower jaw-bone or hard up against your cheek-bone but should be firmly against the fleshy pad of

Most competition shooters adopt a slightly more aggressive stance often with the head slightly lowered before calling a target. This is fine *providing that the same posture is adopted each time.*

Here the head has been pushed over and forward along the comb of the stock. The result is the stock *out on the top of the arm—the shot will probably go left of the target.*

your cheek so that there is a cushion of flesh between the comb of the stock and the angle of your cheek-bone. The top of the comb should run back along your cheek approximately from the corner of your mouth along a line where your teeth meet. The heel of the stock should be level with, or a little below, the top of your shoulder.

The ready position

So how do you go about doing this? As with any action that needs to be repeated consistently well, time and time again, in order to obtain the desired results, a set sequence of events needs to be established. By far the best way to begin this action is to bring the gun into the same basic starting position each time before a shot is taken. If at the same time this starting position is

Bad starting position, safe while the muzzles point at the ground but if this position is adopted when shooting driven game then every time the gun is mounted, the muzzles will come up through the beating line. The gun will start too far behind oncoming targets making a controlled approach along the line difficult and there will be a tendency to intercept crossing and quartering targets.

The basic 'Churchill' style 'ready' position showing square, narrow stance with body weight slightly forward over the balls of both feet. Stock tucked well up under, or into the armpit to encourage the pushing action of the front hand. Head is kept up in a good natural position.

Much safer starting position, muzzles are safely above the cover, but the low stock position will encourage lifting with the rear hand and therefore bad gun mounting.

one which encourages the left arm to push out, and discourages the right one from lifting, then it will go a long way towards making a good mount. Is there such a starting position? The answer of course is 'yes' and it was described a long while ago by Robert Churchill, when he referred to it as the 'ready position' and it has yet to be improved upon. When taking up this starting position, the game shooter in particular must keep safety in mind, and be certain that the gun muzzles never drop below a safe height—that is, not pointing into cover where beaters are working, but always kept pointing safely above the cover at roughly the point you hope to begin the shot. When shooting sporting clays, the muzzles are usually taken back to a point just below the expected line of the target where you intend to begin your swing. As the muzzles are brought safely to the correct starting point, tuck the gun stock quite firmly up under your right arm with the heel of the stock well up into your arm-pit. Allow your right elbow to hang down quite naturally so that the top of the

Good 'ready' position as just described, coupled with good grip and body posture, just prior to mounting the gun.

Mount well under way, the front hand can be seen to be pushing the gun away from the body while picking up the targets flight-line. Head is being kept still.

The completed gun mount. The front hand is still pushing out on the gun. The comb of the stock is firmly up into the pad of the cheek and the shoulder has moved in behind the stock to make a good bed for it. The head is still up and in a good natural position.

Viewed from underneath, good picture of shoulder in behind gun butt to form correct 'pocket'. . .

. . . from above and behind, good finished mount, comb of stock well up into fleshy cheek pad, shoulder well in behind butt, excellent 'shoulder pocket.'

arm traps the stock against your ribs—and you now have the gun in the 'ready position'. At this point I can imagine many game shooters thinking: 'Come on, pull the other one! There's a bird in the air and I have to do all this *before* I mount the gun?' The whole operation, both bringing the muzzles to the correct starting point and tucking the stock up under your arm, takes only a brief moment, and with a little practice becomes an integral part of each shot. Any time lost coming into the 'ready position' is easily made up for in the speed and accuracy of a controlled gun mount.

What are the benefits of this 'ready position'? Firstly it brings your muzzles under control. Secondly, it brings the gun mounting action down to a minimum of movement and, perhaps most important of all, once the stock is tucked up under your right arm, you cannot lift the stock to your cheek and shoulder with your right hand. From this starting position, you have to point or push out with the left hand towards the target sufficiently for the heel of the stock to clear your armpit. As your left hand pushes the gun away from your body, the gun should stay level as it is brought up into your cheek; and as it comes into your cheek, your shoulder moves up and forward in a shrugging motion to lock in against the butt of the stock, to complete the mount. As the gun

moves up from the starting position into the mounted position, the heel just stays in 'brushing contact' with your clothing as your shoulder moves in behind the butt. There is then a moment when everything melds together firmly before the shot is fired. Throughout the whole mounting action your right elbow should remain hanging naturally down; it should not be raised up away from your side as sometimes recommended when bringing up a trap stock to shoot from the 'gun up' position, or when using a rifle. Raising the right elbow during the mount radically changes the shape of the 'shoulder pocket' and can lead to bruising on the inside of the shoulder joint. It also tends to cant the gun over and causes undue strain and tension through the wrist and shoulder.

From start to finish, then, the bulk of the work is done by the left hand and arm and, although both hands have to work in unison as the mount gets under way, the right hand is really being towed along by the left one. As mentioned earlier, the gun should stay level throughout the mount and the right hand should never get above the left. Towards the completion of the mount the right hand exerts a little sideways pressure to help bring the stock firmly against the pad of your cheek and into the shoulder pocket.

Top: *A fine H. Holland double-barrelled 4-bore muzzle loading percussion fowling piece. The 36" barrels of Damascus twist. The gun was originally made in the late 1840s but was discovered in the 1960s 'in the white' (unfinished), and was completed. The address on the top rib is 9 King Street, Holborn, the first address of Harris Holland.*

Bottom: *A 10-bore H Holland double-barrelled muzzle-loading percussion fowling piece with the 9 King Street, Holborn address. Made in 1862 for Captain Turner. This gun, together with the 4-bore percussion, are frequently used in muzzle-loading shooting demonstrations.*

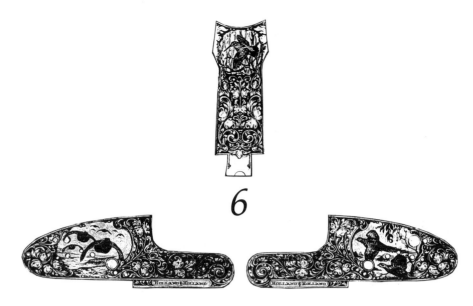

6

Gun Fit

TRADITIONALLY, THE best makers of English guns have long provided a custom-built service for their guns and rifles, either directly through their showrooms, or more satisfactorily through a shooting ground, where customers can be attended by a qualified coach/gun-fitter.

Over the years a 'standard' stock shape has evolved, enabling many makers to build an 'off the shelf' shotgun with the stock finished completely for 'length', 'bend' and 'cast-off'; or with a standard measurement for 'bend' and 'cast-off', but with the stock left so that it can easily be shortened and finished once a customer's correct length has been established. If these 'standard' guns are produced with the classic straight hand stocks, found on most English side-by-side game guns, then small alterations to bend and cast can also be made by setting the stock at the hand, through the use of heat. These guns will prove quite suitable for perhaps seven out of ten of their users—in much the same way as the majority of us can happily wear 'off the peg' clothing, with the occasional help of minor alterations. The remaining minority will be the ones who require much more specialised individual attention to details of fit in order to achieve satisfactory results. Because of extremes of build, eye-sight problems, or perhaps some physical disability, they require a stock length, or amounts of bend or cast, far

removed from the 'norm'. Such bend and cast measurements will have to be built into a stock from the beginning as they cannot normally be obtained through alteration. In some cases modification to fore-end shape, triggers, opening, weight and balance may also be necessary to enable an individual to perform to the best of his/her ability.

At this point it might be as well to try to define 'gun-fit', bearing in mind that our main concern is with game guns, either side-by-side or under-and-over, or with guns used for shooting 'sporting clay pigeons'—in other words, situations where the gun has to be mounted as the shot is taken, and not the 'gun up' trap disciplines. A well-fitting gun is one which can be mounted quickly and easily into the correct position at your cheek and shoulder with little or no conscious effort, throughout the wide range of angles presented by game and sporting clay targets; and when so mounted, points exactly where you look. The gun should come up into your sight-line and there should be no need to drop your head and therefore your sight-line down to meet the gun. Independent head movement is one of the main causes of bad gun mounting. Remember: however well-fitted your gun might be, if you do not mount it correctly, it will not point where you look.

It should be clear from the above that

gun mounting and gun fitting are inextricably linked. An experienced good shot can pick up and use guns with a variety of stock shapes with a fair amount of success, often through making almost unconscious adjustments, though he will never perform quite as well as he would with a gun which fits properly. On the other hand, an inexperienced shot, even with a well-fitting gun, cannot possibly perform consistently until he learns to mount his gun correctly, without having to think about it. In either situation the gun-fitter/coach must be very careful. He must be sure that he is not altering stock shape to compensate for any adjustment (often very subtle) being made by the experienced shot, or for any mistake being made by the inexperienced shot, before making some effort first to correct the mistake. Some mistakes though, through years of practice, may be so ingrained that they are

left to right—

1 Gun stocked to standard bend and cast off, but with stock left unfinished for length.

2 Semi cross-over stock, for someone with central vision, shooting from right shoulder with both eyes open.

3 Full cross-over stock for someone shooting from the right shoulder, using only the left eye.

impossible to correct and eventually may, as a last resort, have to be compensated for in the fitting. This I feel is acceptable, providing that the mistake being made is not causing injury or discomfort, that the mistake has been pointed out and that a serious effort has been made to correct it.

Looking at overall gun fit in more detail, apart from the size, shape, fitness and eye-sight of the individual involved, there are a number of other factors to be taken into consideration, any one of which may have an important bearing on the final stock measurements. These are: barrel length, type of rib, type and length of fore-end, single or double triggers, straight hand stock or some form of pistol-grip, the over-all weight of the finished gun; in addition, the average thickness of clothing worn when using the gun, how far forward an individual feels comfortable with his front hand and where he wishes the gun to balance. Unless otherwise requested, most game guns are normally made to balance at the cross-pin (where the barrels hinge into the knuckle end of the action) leaving the weight of the gun evenly distributed between both hands when it is held correctly. Some users will favour a little more weight in the stock, feeling that this makes the muzzles of the gun more lively; this can work well in some situations but if overdone will make the muzzles unsteady and difficult to control. Others (including many competitive shooters) favour some extra weight forward in the barrels, claiming extra steadiness and a lessened risk of stopping their swing, the extra weight giving some added momentum to the muzzles once they are moving. This again can work well providing it is not overdone to the extent that the muzzles become sluggish to respond at the beginning of the shot, allowing the stock to come up too soon and perhaps too high in the shoulder.

A heavy but well-balanced gun will always handle better than a light but ill-balanced one.

Stock measurements—Basic
Having noted all these individual requirements, three sets of measurements

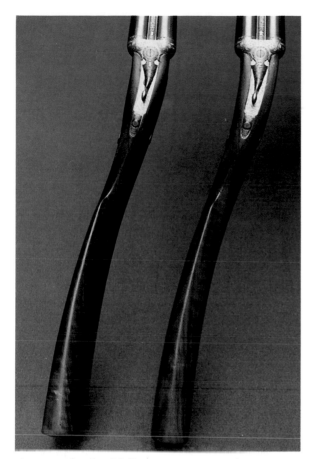

An unusual pair of full cross-over guns, for someone shooting from the left shoulder, but using the right eye.

are needed, from which a new stock can be built, or to which an existing stock can be satisfactorily altered. The measurements required are for length, bend or drop, and cast off or on.

Length is measured from the mid-point of the first or single trigger, to three points on the butt end of the stock. These three points are termed 'heel', 'centre' and 'toe', the main measurement being the one taken at 'centre'.

Bend or **Drop** is the amount which the stock bends or drops down from an imaginary line drawn along the middle of the top-rib and extended out over the top of the stock. It is normally measured at two points, one at either end of the comb of the stock. The two points are the 'bump' (top of heel), and at the other end of the comb near the grip and actually termed 'comb'. As the top of most stocks runs down in a straight line from 'comb' to 'bump' (heel), there is no need to take a separate measurement for

drop at 'face', a term used for a point midway between 'comb' and 'bump' where theoretically the user's cheek is in contact with the stock. In some situations however a Monte Carlo style comb with a step down to the heel may be desirable, when a separate measurement for drop at 'face' is needed.

Cast Off or **On** is the amount which the stock is off-set to one side of that same imaginary line drawn along the middle of the top-rib, either to the right (when viewed from the butt end), and termed 'cast off' for the right-handed user; or to the left for those shooting from the left shoulder, when it is termed 'cast on'.

Four measurements are needed for 'cast' when a new stock is being built. These are taken at 'heel', 'face', 'comb' and 'toe'. If an existing stock is being altered through setting under heat, or sweeping out wood from the blade of the stock, then only one or two measurements are used, those at 'face' and 'heel'.

Taking these three sets of measurements one by one—from records of adult fittings taken over a number of years, some extreme variations have come to light. I have fitted stocks varying in length from 12½ inches at one end of the scale to 17 inches at the other, the main controlling factors here being height, arm length and the thickness of clothing worn when the gun is used. The vast majority of stocks though come out somewhere between 14½ and 14¾ inches at the centre.

The amount of bend or drop in the stock, the measurement which controls the elevation of the shot, can range from a very high (straight) 1¼ inches at the bump (heel), to a low 3 inches or so, but again most stocks finish up measuring somewhere between 2 and 2⅜ inches at this point. As a very general guide here, a short, stocky, square-shouldered person will normally require less drop at heel than will a tall, lean individual with a long neck and sloping shoulders.

The drop measurement at comb varies very little, averaging out at about 1¼ inches.

Cast off or on, depending on which

shoulder you shoot from, starts at a minimal $\frac{1}{16}$ or $\frac{1}{8}$ of an inch at face (no stock is quite dead straight), in an individual of 'normal' build, shooting with the correct eye dominating completely or with the opposite eye closed.

Specialized fitting

Then there is central vision, where the user has both eyes of equal strength yet wishes to shoot with both eyes open. Such a person has no dominant eye, so that their line of sight appears to come from a point midway between the two eyes. The amount of cast required in order to shoot straight using both eyes, will be something in the region of $1\frac{1}{4}$ to $1\frac{3}{4}$ inches at face. Such a stock is termed semi-cross-over.

And finally there is the full cross-over or cross-eyed stock; the user shoots from one shoulder, but with the stock shaped in such a way that it lines up under the opposite eye, which for one reason or another is completely dominant. This is a very specialised fitting, usually for an experienced user who at some point, usually well on in his shooting career, has lost the sight in what may previously have been his master eye and so opts for the cross-over stock rather than learning to shoot again from the other shoulder. It is a difficult fitting to make, and never an easy gun to use, but in the right hands can be very successful. The amount of cast

Just two examples of different physical features which could require specialist fitting.
The man on the left would probably need less bend, but a little more cast than the man on the right.
Note different face shapes, neck lengths, and shoulder slopes.

No matter how well fitted the gun might be, you still have to mount it correctly.

required in such a stock is usually between $2\frac{1}{2}$ and $3\frac{1}{4}$ inches at face.

These extremes of cast are normally only found in side-by-side game guns, very rarely in under-and-over guns, many users with opposite eye problems preferring to close or somehow mask the opposite eye, or, if this is a problem that is discovered from the outset rather than one which develops as the years go by, to learn to shoot from the other shoulder.

Eye-sight—Eye dominance

Eye-sight is extremely variable and peculiarly personal, not only changing gradually in most of us as the years go by, but in some changing quite markedly from day to day, usually through some form of fatigue. I have seen the same person shoot on two consecutive days where on the first day he shot well and was completely right eye dominant and on the second day completely left eye dominant. It turned out that he had sat up very late working the night before the second session and had had a fairly long drive to get to the school on the second day. Whatever the cause, the effect was disastrous. Such sudden marked changes are usually temporary and revert after a good night's rest. They are usually brought about by such things as a long car drive, or through doing a lot of close-up work such as reading, writing or something similar, where the eye which normally dominates apparently becomes tired and appears to switch off, allowing the other to take over for a period.

The dominant or master eye is not necessarily the one through which you see best, but rather the one which focuses first. Normally when we look at any object with both eyes, one will focus before the other and it is this eye, the one which focuses first, that controls the line of a shot, even though you may actually see more clearly through the other one.

The first reaction of many right-handers on discovering, or being shown, that they have a dominant left eye, particularly if they already wear prescription glasses for shooting, is to rush to their optician in order to have a correction made. I have yet to see this work. Prescription lenses can of course improve your distance vision by bringing things back into sharp focus, but they do not appear to change the speed at which each eye focuses, and therefore which eye dominates through focusing first. It seems the best that can be done if you use glasses, but do not wish to, or indeed are unable to close the left eye, is to use some device to interfere with the sharp focusing of the left eye. Here you may have to go through a certain amount of trial and error until you come up with the solution that suits you best.

Although there is no doubt that the ideal way to shoot a shotgun at moving targets is with both eyes open, always providing that you have the correct dominant eye, or that the gun has been otherwise fitted to enable you to do so. For many people with opposite eye dominance the easiest solution is to close, or part close in order to fade, the opposite eye as the gun is mounted. This should force the eye over the rib of the gun to focus on the target.

The ability of people with opposite eye dominance to close the dominant eye and allow the other eye to work is extremely varied, as is the amount which the eye has to be closed in order to effect this change

over. For some, nothing short of clamping the eye tightly closed will work, as the slightest degree of peeking through the opposite eye will be sufficient to pull the shot off line. For others, all that is needed is a partial shading of the eye through hooding the eye-lid in order to allow the eye over the gun to take over completely.

Some people when asked to close the opposite eye, find it to be a very simple and effective solution, suffering no handicap at all, being able to pick up targets with both eyes open, closing the offending eye as the gun is mounted, and very quickly learn to do it without thinking. Others will find it difficult to do this initially, finding at first that there is perhaps an increased tendency to look back at the rib of the gun before shooting. Normally this can soon be overcome with a little practice in mounting the gun onto a chosen aim-mark and learning the eye closing at the same time, again until it can be done without thinking. Whenever you practise mounting your gun, always pick out a particular point (aim-mark) at which to look. If you simply mount the gun into the sky all you will be doing is practising looking at the gun! To help avoid the temptation of glancing back at the gun before shooting, the old trick of pin-pointing a particular spot on the target, rather than the target as a whole, will help.

On the other hand there will be some who, when asked to close the opposite eye, will find it completely impossible, at least initially, to do so. They are so dominant in the one eye that the other is hardly being used. They can usually close the eye that you want them to keep open and use, very easily, but when asked to close the other (strongly dominant) eye, find that both eyes will close at the same time; they cannot close the dominant eye on its own. To some extent this can be overcome with practice, but it will never prove easy. For anyone falling into this last category some other solution may have to be sought. Much will depend on the individual involved, on what sort of shooting he or she wishes to do and just how determined they are to do it. If the whole thing is just for the occasional outing, shooting some

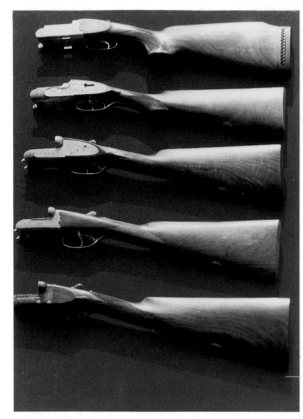

A selection of different stock styles.
Top to bottom.

1 Under-and-over with Monte Carlo comb, single-trigger full pistol grip and ventilated recoil-pad.

2 Under-and-over game gun with double triggers and semi-pistol grip.

3 Standard stock on side-by-side game gun.

4 20 bore side-by-side lady's game gun with stock shortened and 'toe' of stock rounded off for comfort, though she declined a recoil-pad.

5 12 bore game gun with standard bend and cast, but with stock not yet finished for length.

fairly straightforward clay targets with a small group of friends, then by wearing a pair of glasses (prescription, if worn, shooting or sun glasses) with the lens over the opposite eye covered, or part covered, with tape or something similar, in order to block out the eye they cannot close, they can often perform well enough with the one eye to enjoy reasonable success and perhaps be encouraged enough to take things a step further.

This patching over of the opposite eye can work very well in some cases, indeed with regular practice and some careful

experimenting the actual patch on the lens can often be refined to a comparatively small area providing that it is positioned accurately and that the glasses are well fitting enough not to move as shots are taken. If this happens the patch will suddenly cease to be effective as the eye begins to see around it. To position the patch correctly you need to enlist the aid of a helper who can stand alongside and half facing you, on the side opposite the shoulder you are shooting from. For this first trial the best thing to use as a patch is a small circular 'peel off' label, or target patch, of the type readily available in strips or sheets, and each about the size of a one pound coin. If not stuck down too firmly on the lens to begin with they can easily be peeled off again and re-positioned if need be. It may be necessary to add a second patch to extend the height, depth or width of the first in order to create an effective block out to begin with.

Wearing the chosen glasses, carefully check that the gun you are going to use is empty. Take up a good stance and bring the gun into the described 'ready' position. With your helper alongside armed with a sticky patch, pick out an 'aiming mark' at about eye-level somewhere straight ahead. Now keeping both eyes open, concentrate on the chosen mark and mount the gun onto it. Hold the position while your helper carefully positions a patch on the lens centring it over the pupil of the offending eye. Take down the gun and re-mount it two or three times onto your chosen mark and you should be able to judge quite well for yourself whether or not the patch is placed correctly, or whether it needs re-positioning because you can see around it. It is important that you conduct this test with the gun mounted correctly as you will find that you will be looking through a different portion of the lens than you would if you simply tried to place a patch on the lens yourself with the glasses in position, but without the gun.

Once you are happy that the patch is effective in blocking out the opposite eye, and after proving it with some shooting at targets you feel are within your ability, you may find that you can reduce the size or shape of the patch to make it less obtrusive. Depending upon how much shooting you go on to do you may also find that you can progress from an opaque patch to a translucent one (a couple of layers of clear adhesive tape can eventually be sufficient, just enough to blur the eye and prevent it from focusing on the target). Other alternatives which can work well are a smear of petroleum jelly, or a dab of lipstick or lip-salve spread over the correct area with a finger-tip. Once happy in your own mind that you have chosen the most suitable remedy for this eye problem you may feel that you would like a more permanent arrangement. There are adhesive translucent patches on the market designed to stick onto the inside surface of your lens, made in a variety of colours to match the colours of the various lenses available for shooting glasses; or you may even choose to have a permanent 'frosted' patch ground or etched onto the lens by your optician.

For anyone wanting to shoot seriously and discovering early on that they have the wrong eye strongly dominant, providing you are prepared to put in some dedicated, initial practice (and this really will mean some hard work to begin with), it may well be worth your while learning to shoot from the other shoulder, when you will be able to use your master eye over the gun and probably keep both eyes open. When this alternative is offered as a solution the first reaction may be very negative, as early attempts to change shoulders (and of course to reverse your stance and hand positions on the gun) will feel very difficult and poorly co-ordinated, but with a little perseverance things will quickly improve. There is no good reason why you should not shoot as well as anyone else once you overcome the initial awkwardness of the change over.

This alternative will not work well for anyone with central vision, as which ever shoulder you shoot from, if you wish to keep both eyes open, you will probably need as much cast off from one as you will need cast on from the other.

There have been a number of things tried in the past as an alternative to either casting the gun stock or closing an eye. There are various attachments which are either screwed onto or slip over the top rib or barrels of the gun. All work to some extent, even if only on certain shots. They range from a 'Perspex' muzzle attachment which has on it a short 'arm' in the top of which is drilled a series of holes into which a fairly large bead can be threaded to act as a reference point. Fire a series of shots at a fixed mark, moving the bead along the series of holes until, when using this movable bead as your reference point (instead of the normal bead at the muzzle end of the rib), you are placing your shot straight on the aim-mark. The movable bead can then be screwed or glued into the correct hole in the attachment once a straight line to the target has been established. Or you can use a complete extra top rib with front bead, clamped to lie like an out-rigger along one side of, but several inches away from, the barrels. This extra rib is then used instead of the normal top rib when a shot is made. Its correct position has again to be found by trial and error. The whole arrangement is rather flimsy, but I have seen it work.

Another is the so-called left eye 'blot-out' or 'blinder'. Looking rather like one of Mickey Mouse's ears, it is slipped over the barrels on an elasticated band, or may be attached to a hand guard. When positioned correctly it comes up in front of the opposite eye as the gun is mounted. I have not seen this attachment work well other than on targets flying fairly directly away from the gun. On most targets, by the time the 'blot-out' becomes effective (really only once the gun is fully mounted) it is too late and the eye has already pulled the shot off line. If you like gadgets you may wish to try one or all of these alternatives in order to satisfy your curiosity. One big disadvantage with all of them is that they have to be removed each time the gun is put away into a cover or gun case.

One last point on opposite eye dominance before moving on. The majority of right-handed men have dominant right eyes at least until middle/late middle age, when they may suddenly experience a complete change over in master eye as their

From a coach's eye view, two instances of fitting problems.

When mounted correctly this gun (above) will shoot very low as there is an excessive amount of drop/bend in the stock (not to be confused with a stock mounted too high in the shoulder, which would give a similar picture).

View (below) showing dominant left eye over gun causing shots to go well to the left side of targets.

eye-sight weakens. The overwhelming majority of right-handed women however are left eye dominant, often very strongly so. I would put the percentage at 85/90%. As a result very few can shoot successfully from the right shoulder with a standard stocked gun *unless they close or blot out the left eye.* Many women have been

discouraged from shooting by their lack of success brought about through being told that they have to keep both eyes open in order to shoot well with a shotgun. For most right-handed women nothing could be further from the truth. Without a complicated fitting or changing to the opposite shoulder, almost all would be better off shooting with the left eye closed, or with a patch in the correct spot on their shooting glasses.

Although eye-sight, or perhaps I should say eye dominance, plays a large part in deciding the necessary amount of cast required in a stock in order to shoot straight with both eyes open, it is not the only controlling factor. In order to get a straight line from gun to target, the leading eye has of course to be directly over the top-rib, and here the shape of your face can have a bearing on the amount of cast required in order to get that straight line. Normally a minimal amount of cast, coupled with the stance described earlier and perhaps a slight turn of the head towards the stock, will put the eye directly over the top-rib. But, for those of you with very full or wide faces, some added cast may be important. Anyone with chubby cheeks or a wide lower jaw may need more than what would be called a normal or standard cast to achieve that sought-after straight line, even though there is no doubt about the dominant eye. Indeed in some individuals where a wide face is coupled with closely set eyes it may be necessary to give a good ½ inch or more of cast at the face of the stock, in order to get that eye directly over the top rib.

Basic gun fitting
It may be enlightening if at this point I take you through the basic principles of a typical fitting for an all-round game gun or one suitable for shooting sporting clays. The assumption here is that at least part of the session is with a 'try-gun', either in side-by-side or under-and-over.

On first meeting the person concerned and establishing which shoulder he or she shoots from, the try-gun is set up initially through taking an educated guess at a suitable stock length, having judged their height and build by eye and by adjusting the stock to give a near standard amount of bend and cast at heel. This first stage is often done indoors, with perhaps an adjustment to stock length after watching the gun being mounted once or twice, and after ascertaining how the amount and thickness of clothing being worn compares with what will normally be worn on shooting days. (The experienced shots will of course bring their regular gear with them for a fitting.)

Next a few minutes will be spent at the fitting plates where gun handling and mounting can be watched in more detail. Any glaring mistakes made are pointed out and hopefully corrected as little progress can be made until the gun is being mounted reasonably well. At this stage, and before any shots have been fired, further alteration may be made to stock length, and all the while I will be looking for 'feed-back' from the client. I need to quickly establish a rapport, hopefully within a minute or two of our first meeting, in order that we get the best from one another. Through the session I need to be asking questions, encouraging comment, looking out for reactions, good or bad, changes in attitude or posture as any alterations are made to the gun. I need to gain and hold onto a person's trust, their confidence in me and what I am doing in order to get over the almost inevitable bad patch when things go wrong, usually because one or both of us is trying too hard. At this stage it becomes all too easy to start blaming the gun or the size and shape I have made it. Having adjusted the stock to a comfortable length and with the gun mounting going along reasonably well, the next stage is to establish whether one or both eyes are to be used and, if both, whether or not there are any problems concerning eye dominance. There are many tests for finding out which is your master eye; most entail pointing a finger at, or mounting the gun onto a mark while keeping both eyes open. Hold the position just for a moment, still concentrating on the chosen aim-mark, then either close or get someone to cover over the opposite eye. If all is well then as the other eye is closed or

covered, the gun muzzle will continue to point at or very close to the mark. If, as the eye is closed or covered, the muzzles of the gun are found to jump appreciably off to one side then there is normally a problem with the opposite eye wanting to dominate. I do not think that any one of these tests is infallible. The only real test is to fire a series of shots with the gun well mounted at straight oncoming and straight going away targets. This will tell much more than any of the commonly used pointing tests at stationary marks. Even here though a few people will run into trouble and cause the coach a real headache. They may shoot well on straight targets with both eyes open with no apparent problems, but if shooting from the right shoulder when presented with a quartering shot on the left side, either going away or oncoming, will suddenly start shooting well to the left (or in front) of these targets, the left eye apparently taking over on these narrow angles. I have seen this happen on a number of occasions and before anyone says they know the answer, let me say that it was not just because the turn to the left is easy for right-handers, which sometimes leads to interception of close targets on the left; or that they were eclipsing the right eye as the gun was mounted. Those concerned were firing genuine left-eye shots just on those narrow angles, the wider crossing shots not being a problem. Two common factors are noticeable in these individuals. The first is that their eyes are set fairly wide apart; the second is that they display a reluctance to turn their bodies for these shots, preferring to do most of the work with their arms. This latter fact can naturally lead to the stock coming away from the cheek as the shot is fired which can cause the shot to go to the left, but there is more to it than that. With wide-set eyes, and by inclining the head slightly to the right ready to receive the gun-stock, the left eye becomes higher than the right one so that these particular targets may be seen first through the left eye, if the body is not turned; then the left eye continues to control the shot causing a miss well to the left of the target.

Once made aware of the problem, two

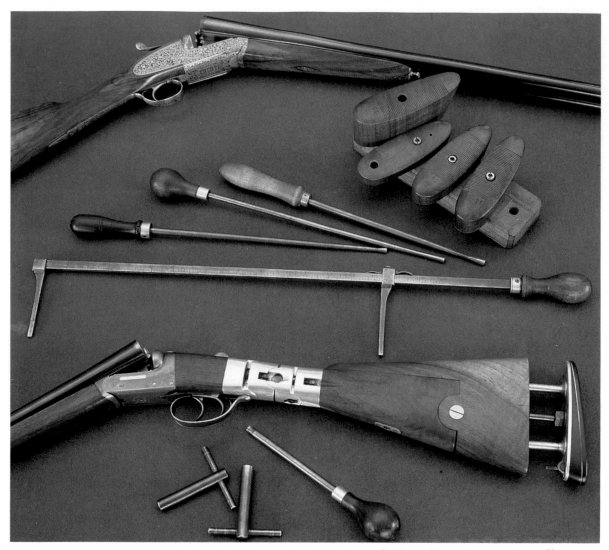

Try gun and tools used to assess correct length, bend and cast.

things may help on these angles: one is to take a little more time, if available, at the start to ensure that both eyes see the target as it appears and to make certain that the muzzles pick up its line correctly from just behind; secondly, if this does not work, to shade down the left eye by part-closing it, to make certain that the right eye controls the shot from the beginning.

Let's go back now to the client waiting patiently at the fitting-plates. The try-gun has been set up with a comfortable-looking stock length, bend and cast are standard, and there are no major eye-sight problems. If I now feel it necessary, I ask if he or she would mind pointing the gun at me once or twice. This request is often met with a look of horror or disbelief, as we are about to break the first rule of shooting, and if

someone flatly refuses as occasionally happens then I must respect their wishes. Usually though, after explaining why this is desirable, and having checked carefully that the gun is empty (several times!), I can move out just in front of the gun and while checking that the stock is coming nicely up into the cheek and shoulder, ask him/her to look at and point the gun at my right eye. When all is well I want to see their shooting eye directly over and just a little above the top rib and I may now have to make small adjustments to the bend and/or cast measurement of the stock to achieve this picture. Once this stage is reached two or three shots are fired at a mark on the plate at about eye level, from a distance of 25 yards or so. If the mounting is consistent then the shots should arrive one on top of the other, and if the fitting is reasonable the shots should naturally be good and straight but hopefully about two-thirds of the charge will be above the mark. If not, then further small adjustments may be made to the stock and two or three more shots taken. Too much time spent on the plate at this stage can be counter-productive as, when shooting a shotgun at a fixed mark, most people quickly become too conscious of what they are doing and shooting at a fixed mark will not necessarily give the same result as shooting at a moving target. For example, some people will appear to be completely left eye dominant on a fixed mark (possibly because of the added amount of time they have to take the shots), but will prove to be right eye dominant with moving targets where their response is more instinctive.

A number of shots at a medium, straight, oncoming target should ascertain whether or not further adjustment to the cast measurement is called for, but the real test will be on straight going away targets. To check elevation, and therefore bend measurement, the straight going away shot is important, as are some quartering and crossing shots on both sides. All the way through the session the gun handling and mounting should be carefully monitored in order to get consistent results. At the end of the session if the client is reasonably experienced we should have a good set of measurements. If on the other hand most of the session has been spent going over basic gun handling techniques and making corrections, then it may be essential to have at least one more session to prove a fitting.

A compromise situation

For anyone shooting game or sporting clays gun-fit will of necessity always be something of a compromise, firstly because of the wide variety of target heights, angles, speeds and distances both will be presented with, and secondly because of the wide range of conditions they may find themselves shooting under. All must be taken into consideration for the final fitting. For example, the man who walks up grouse over dogs in late August, or waits in a midge-laden butt in early September for grouse to come skimming in low over the heather, or perhaps for the sudden appearance of partridges bursting over a

hedge-top may well be shooting almost in shirt-sleeves; but the same man with the same gun will want to be able to use it with similar efficiency when wrapped up well against the wind and rain while shooting high pheasants in December and January, or waiting for pigeons to come to roost in February and March. From this it should be plain that ideal stock length is perhaps the most difficult measurement to assess, and if in any doubt it is far better to err slightly on the short side than on the long side, in order to accommodate winter clothing and permit the quick yet smooth gun mounting called for on certain shots.

Care must be taken during a fitting to view shots made at a variety of heights and angles, again remembering that most shooting people will wish to use the same gun(s) for several different types of shooting. For example, here in the U.K. the season may well start with shots at very low elevations with walked-up, and driven grouse, move on through driven partridges and medium pheasants and culminate with very high pheasants as the season draws to a close. In the U.S.A. similarly, the same gun may well be used on low-flying quail and high flying doves. Due consideration then must be given to comb height for all around shooting. For instance, it is no good fitting a high-combed stock, which may well give excellent results on high driven birds by providing a built-in lead, only to find that the gun then places the shot charge way over the top of low, going away, oncoming and crossing targets such as grouse, quail or rabbits. On the other hand, unless the gun is to be used for no other purpose, a low comb may well give good results on walked-up shots, but place the shot too low to be satisfactory on high oncoming and passing shots. So, a happy medium must be sought for general use.

After the initial fitting, as the years go by, eye-sight weakens, sometimes bringing about a complete change in 'master eye', calling for a major change in technique or stock shape. Body weight can vary and body posture changes, becoming gradually more stooping. Minor changes to stock length, bend or cast may be necessary in order to maintain your performance.

A rare 10-bore black powder gold inlaid double-barrelled rifle No. 8266 made in 1884 for His Exalted Highness the Nizam Hyderabad.

*The efficiency of any ear-muffs relies very much upon the soft padded area of the muff sitting snugly to form a good seal around each ear. This seal though can so easily be made inefficient by wearing the muffs over a bulky cap, long hair, or glasses with wide side-pieces. For the same reason you should not try to straighten out the head band of the muffs as it is this that applies the necessary inward pressure to each muff to form an efficient seal. Muffs should fit comfortably and snugly and should not slip off as you shoot.

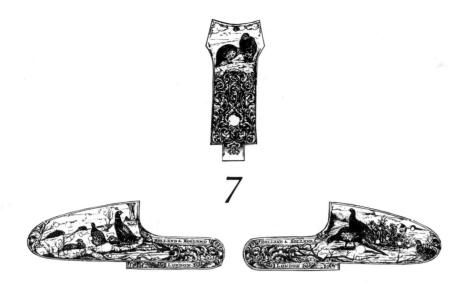

7

Target 'Pick Up'

WHETHER SHOOTING game or clay targets, often the first warning you get when waiting to shoot will be the sound (wing-beats or a call) of birds in the air or the noise made by the trap as it launches a target. This will of course depend very much upon your own hearing ability and the type of hearing protection being worn. Some game shooters find solid plugs a hindrance in situations where they rely very much on hearing birds before seeing them, or upon heeding a warning whistle or call from a neighbour or beater as birds approach an unsighted peg or butt. In such situations a pair of ear-muffs with a built-in amplification system, which can be switched on or off, can help, especially if you are hard of hearing anyway. Such muffs worn properly* not only offer good protection by effectively blocking out harmful gun shot noise, but also amplify low level sound so that the approach of birds and animals (not to mention the gossip of other guns!) can be heard more clearly than with the 'naked ear'.

On the other hand many competition shooters may well wear both plugs and muffs in an effort to cut out all external noise, firstly as an aid to concentration, and secondly so that they do not become reliant on the sound of a trap going off, but rather on the sight of the target (as the rules require) to begin each shot. It can be quite a shock to move from a familiar competition field where, without even realising it, you have become used to reacting to the sound of the traps going off to another using quieter traps where you suddenly realise that you have been relying on your ears rather than your eyes and that you are responding to the targets five yards later than usual. As a result your timing will suffer badly.

If shooting competitively then, when you will often be relying solely on your eyesight to first pick up each target, you must assess each situation carefully as you move from stand to stand and consider how to best set yourself up for the targets presented in order to perform well. Hopefully, at each stand, you will have the opportunity to watch several others shoot before your turn comes, or at the very least if you are first to shoot you should be given the chance to see the targets thrown once, so that you know their trajectories and can decide where you intend taking the shots. Having decided how and where to take the shots will largely govern the way you set your feet (see section on stance). Just remember to keep your stance relaxed and fairly narrow, with your feet placed in such a way that you can let your weight go towards the target and that you can turn freely for crossing shots.

Starting-point—muzzles
The next decision is perhaps the most

It is hoped that at each stand, you will have the opportunity to watch several others shoot before your turn comes . . .

important of all to make each time you set yourself up to take a shot, and that is where to point your gun-muzzles before calling for the target(s); in other words where best to pick up the target with the gun-muzzles (or if you prefer, with your leading hand) so that you can get onto its line and so judge its speed correctly. As described earlier in the 'Method', the most certain way for most people to judge both the line and speed of any target is to pick it up from behind, that is to get your gun-muzzles onto the line along which the target has just travelled and to complete the shot by moving the muzzles smoothly through the target as the shot is fired. This statement begs three questions:

How far behind the target do I start?
When do I mount the gun?
How far through the targets do I have to go?

Unfortunately, there is no straightforward answer to any of these questions. We are back to those basic guide-lines. Remember that each one of us sees things slightly differently, that reaction times differ from one to the other and that different guns handle in different ways.

Differing barrel-lengths
For example, generally speaking, light, short-barrelled guns are fast to handle but can be hard to control as they may come onto a target quickly; by the same token they will also go off it quickly. In some situations this fast handling can be an advantage, as when standing in a grouse butt for instance with birds often appearing with little warning and where, for safety reasons, there is a limited amount of space to make the shots, or when walking up birds in thick cover, where anything flushed may at best give only the most fleeting of chances before putting a tree between itself and you and is gone. In both these situations the good shots are usually quick and instinctive though not rushed, calling for accurate gun mounting without any prolonged swing. These shots, and you will of course come across similar targets on some sporting clay stands, are often referred to as 'snap' or 'spot' shooting, but if watched carefully, with the possible exception of a target flying straight away at eye-level, it will be seen that the gun is still brought onto and through the bird from behind. The swing may be very short with the muzzles starting on the bird's tail and the shot fired as they pass the beak, so that the feeling may well be one of shooting right at the bird. Nevertheless this is still a swing through, even though the gun-muzzles only travel through a few inches.

At the other end of the scale, heavier, longer barrelled guns are slower to respond at the beginning of a shot, calling for a little more initial effort to start them moving (a possible disadvantage in the type of shot just described) but, once moving, tend to keep going under their own momentum and are much easier to control (to keep moving steadily) on high overhead and long crossing shots where there is a lot of time to see the bird and where a longer more deliberate swing through is called for. Between these two extremes are all the variations of line, speed and distance (and therefore the amount of time available for the shot) found with live quarry and with targets presented around good sporting clays courses.

How far behind?

Back to the question, 'How far behind the target do I start?' The answer is just far enough behind it to get a good feeling for its line and speed before swinging smoothly through to shoot. Start too close to the target and you will catch and overtake it too quickly without having had time to judge line and speed correctly, or without the gun being fully mounted. Results will be inconsistent and many

---

NOTE

It is far easier to pick up the line of any crossing, quartering, low going away, or low oncoming targets by holding the muzzles slightly below the expected flight line as you call your target. There is no risk then of the target being obscured from your view by the muzzles and it is much easier to pick up the line of any of these targets by coming onto it from slightly below rather than by trying to drop onto the line from above. With a pair of crossing targets coming out one above the other it is usually easier to take the lower one first, then, with the second target still in view above the gun, to come onto its line from below. Take the higher one first and you may have difficulty finding the line of the second target as it is now somewhere below your gun-muzzles. Remember also that many game and sporting clays guns are made or fitted to throw their patterns a little high, so that by coming onto the line of a crossing or quartering bird from just below, then pushing through the bottom edge of the target as it were, that there is no time during such a shot when you need lose sight of and there-fore your concentration on, the target.

---

shots will be late through having to make corrections in order to compensate for the bad start made too close to the target.

On the other hand if you start too far behind the target, if you let it make too much ground on you before starting after it, your swing along the target's flight line will be hurried and out of control as you struggle to overtake it. In extreme examples of this some people will mount their gun with the muzzles travelling backwards along the target's line towards its starting point, then stop and begin moving the other way to chase after and eventually over-haul it at high speed in the mistaken belief that this practice helps them to swing well.

With clay targets, having decided where to take your first shot (remembering that on many sporting clay stands you will also have a second target to deal with and that this may have an important bearing on deciding where you should take the first), you should take the gun-muzzles back to point along and *just below* (see also note in box on this page) the position on the expected flight line where you wish to begin the shot and where you can see the target clearly, not just as an orange or black blur as it first leaves the trap or clears cover.

. . . or if you are first to shoot you should be given the chance to see the targets thrown once.

Bolting rabbit target—left-handed Shooter.
1 *Gun in 'ready position', muzzles well back towards trap (natural swing left to right when shooting from the left shoulder), and just below level of run. Body weight already forward over front foot as target is called for.*

3 *Gun stock coming well up into cheek as muzzles catch up with target. Right arm now nicely extended, body continues to turn to face target squarely.*

2 *Target appears, muzzles begin to pick up its line and speed from just behind; this is being done with the right hand as it begins to push forward to mount the gun. Body beginning to turn with weight going towards target.*

4 *Muzzles follow through target as shot is fired. Body continues to turn with weight still pivoting well forward over front foot.*

Keep your stance relaxed and fairly narrow so that you can let your weight go towards the target or turn freely for crossing shots.

For some of you with eagle eyes and fast reactions this may mean all the way back to the trap; for others with less sharp eyes and slower reactions the best position to start may well be at a point about midway along the line between the place you first see the target and the spot you wish to take the shot. Do not be afraid to experiment if you find you are lagging behind your target and feel as though you are having to hurry and chase after it. Try starting a little further out from the trap. If on the other hand you find that you are catching the target very quickly and that you are having to 'dab the brakes' as you shoot or that you have a feeling that you are intercepting rather than following it, then take your muzzles closer to the target's starting point. This last problem, that of catching up with the target too quickly, is quite common with right-handed shooters when dealing with targets crossing or quartering to their left. This situation is of course reversed for the left handed shooter when dealing with similar targets to the right.

This is one situation where it does not help to stand facing too far round towards the point you wish to take the shot, advice often given and accepted without question when shooting clay targets. If you do it is difficult to bring the muzzles far enough back along the expected flight line in order to pick up the target correctly. This being the natural turn for the right-hander you are normally better off taking the muzzles further back towards the target's starting point to make certain you can start behind it than you are if you start with the muzzles too far out along the target's line. The fact that this is the natural turn for the right-hander does not necessarily make it an easy shot. Turning your stance to face the point you wish to take the shot, and then winding the muzzles back along the line to the correct pick-up point so that you can unwind as the shot is taken usually comes into its own with targets crossing or quartering to the right. This is an unnatural turn, against the body, where most right-handers need all the help they can get and even then will still have to work a little harder than they do on the left side. In view of this be careful not to start or get left too

Follow the gun muzzles up towards the top right corner of the picture and you will see the target just a moment before it is shot. Orange target quartering away right to left. Gun stock is well mounted just before target is overtaken. In the picture below the target is well hit, gun muzzles have followed through, but the stock and cheek have perhaps parted company a little early.

far behind the target at the beginning of such shots. I still haven't really answered the question, 'How far behind the target do I start?' As a guide, the nearer to you a target is, or the faster it is going, then the closer to it you start. This usually means putting the muzzles onto the target's line no more than two or three feet behind it, completing the mounting action just before catching up with it and moving smoothly

Approaching a low going away target by coming up along the flight-line from below. Although there doesn't seem to be much doubt from the very business-like mount that he will break the target, has he got left just a little bit far behind it by perhaps mounting the stock too soon?

With a pair of crossing targets coming out one above the other (these two are crossing from left to right), it is usually easier to take the lower one first, then with the second target still in view above the gun, to come on to its line from below.

through to take the shot with the swing unchecked as, and for a moment after, the shot is taken.

With high targets seen coming from any distance or with long crossing targets the first thing that becomes obvious is the added amount of time there is to take the shot, the length of time you have to watch the target in the air before shooting it. Such shots are difficult to pace correctly, perhaps even more so with game than clay targets where birds can sometimes be seen flying for several hundred yards before coming into range, something not yet possible with artificial targets. The best (or perhaps the worst!) that can be done with a clay pigeon is to start it a hundred yards or so from the

Taking the muzzles back to the point you first pick up the target clearly. The right-handed shooter will turn naturally for the high quartering away target from right to left. The left-handed shooter, however, already has his body turned towards his 'killing area' ready to unwind on what is his unnatural swing.

gun and have it come dropping in losing height and speed quickly as it comes into range some way out in front of the shooter. The difficulty is knowing when and where to begin these shots. Game shooters try all sorts of ploys in an effort to make shots at such targets as instinctive or as natural as possible; they will see the birds coming and then purposely look away, usually down at the ground or at their boots, looking up only when they feel the bird will be close enough to take in one single smooth action, incorporating the correct approach along the bird's line, accurate gun mounting and a good follow through. Another trick used is that of mounting the gun twice, going through a false mounting action onto the bird just before it enters the shooting zone, bringing the gun down from the shoulder back into the 'ready' position and then straightaway starting the pick-up of the bird's line and the gun mount again in an effort to make as natural

a shot as possible. None of these ways though is really suitable for shooting clay targets, where the whole thing really becomes a matter of discipline. You need to be certain in your own mind where you intend taking the shot and how far back along the line you must go in order to pick up the target correctly with the muzzles before calling for each target. Having called the target this is when you need the discipline not to begin too soon but to let the target come on towards your starting point before beginning to push out the front hand to start your mount and movement along the line. The whole action may seem to be taking place in slow motion and you need to be careful during this first stage as you are bringing the muzzles onto the target's line that you do not overtake it too soon or get the stock fully mounted too early. There may well be a period when the gun-muzzles are moving along the flight line just behind and at the same speed as the target with the stock as yet not fully up into your cheek or shoulder. As the shot nears completion (as the target approaches the point at which you have decided to shoot it) the stock is firmly mounted as the muzzles swing through the target to give the necessary lead. There may again be a

Not much doubt as to which one of this pair of 'springing teal' has been chosen first . . .

. . . here, though, the two targets appearing very close together in the top left corner are plainly unscathed by the first shot. This pair is crossing and dropping from left to right. In such a situation, especially if the two targets cross over during their flight it can be very difficult to separate them in your mind and give each in turn your full attention. Two other possible reasons for the miss are: not taking the muzzles far enough back towards the trap (it looks as though the shot missed in front even though this is the awkward swing) and note the high right elbow—perhaps she killed them both with her second shot.

Left: With high targets seen coming from any distance, the first thing that becomes obvious is the added time you have to see the bird before shooting.

moment when this lead (your correct sight picture) is held for a moment, with the muzzles moving at the same speed as, but now ahead of, the target before the shot is taken. Now, how do you define that? Maintained approach, follow through *and* maintained lead, all in one shot! How far you start behind these longer targets is very much a matter of experience, but it is usually two to three times the distance you would start behind the closer, quicker, more instinctively shot targets. The biggest

'How far ahead of the target do I have to go?' This picture was taken (accidentally) just a split second before the pheasant was cleanly killed. It clearly shows the shot string on its way to the bird, and for any disbelievers who say it's not possible to see the shot charge, look again.

For a low going away shot, keep the muzzles low so that the target's line can be picked up with the eyes and then the muzzles as it appears rising above the gun.

Not a good starting position—the target will appear below the gun—you may not see it clearly and will have to drop down onto it so that target and muzzles will be moving in opposite directions.

problem with these long shots is normally the increased amount of time you have to watch them. The hardest thing to do is to keep your concentration on the target, especially when in such situations you have to become aware of the fact that you are clearly holding the muzzles ahead of the target in order to hit it. At these longer ranges the gun muzzles are often moving comparatively slowly, as a movement of a few inches at the muzzles is covering many yards along the target's line. As you open up the gap between the target and the muzzles you must keep your full concentration on the target itself and not let it wander to the gun or the actual gap or you will simply stop your swing. Everything happens at a slower pace than it does with closer, faster targets so you need to be more conscious of keeping the gun moving as and after you fire the shot.

When to mount

The one big advantage of starting just behind the target is that by mounting the gun accurately onto its exact trajectory one can only miss behind or in front. Trying to maintain a lead (especially with game-birds), or directly approaching crossing targets at an angle of 45° from below, will also cause misses either underneath or above.

I am not condemning these other methods—each will work well for some of you in certain situations—but after watching thousands of shooters firing millions of cartridges over the past 26 years, the 'follow through' method has proved far and away the most consistent and successful for the large majority of users.

In answering the first question, I have also partly answered the second: 'When do I mount the gun?' Asked more correctly the question I think should be, 'When do I complete the gun mount?' As stated earlier, if the stock is fully mounted too soon, it then becomes difficult to swing freely as you will already be tensing up to take the recoil; if fully mounted too late then there is the danger of firing the shot before everything comes solidly together. The mount begins, albeit slowly, as soon as you

begin to pick up the line of the target with the muzzles, because the same action, that of beginning to push or point the left hand out towards the target is doing both things, bringing the gun up into your sight-line as it moves the muzzles along the line the target has just flown. The stock should become fully mounted, that is, be firmly up into the pad of your cheek, with your shoulder locking everything together just before you move through the target and the position should be held for a moment after firing the shot as you follow through.

How much lead

As for the third question, 'How far through the target do I have to go?', there truly is no straightforward answer. This is where through practice you really must build your own answers, your own sight pictures, remembering that what you see when you hit a target need not be what anyone else sees when they shoot at a similar target. These sight pictures, this necessary amount of 'lead' or 'forward allowance' that you will find you must give to certain targets in order to hit them, should wherever possible be learned by experience so that it becomes instinctive rather than calculated.

The best I can do for you here, almost in the form of a re-cap, is to bring together some of the points made earlier, by going over some of the basic guide-lines.

Firstly let's talk about those targets which for most shooters do not require a conscious 'lead'. (Remembering two things: most guns used in game and sporting clay shooting are fitted purposely to throw their patterns a little high, and secondly that we are usually dealing with 'gun down' situations where the stock is brought up when the target appears, not 'gun up' situations as used in the various trap shooting disciplines.)

The first of these targets is one getting up ahead of you and flying straight away at, or below, eye level. This is where you need to shoot at the legs or the bottom edge of the target. Keep it in view as you shoot it. If you are doing everything correctly there should be no need to cover the target with the gun. Not only is your gun going to purposely throw its charge a little high, but

In this sporting clay situation with a pair of 'springing teal' rising quickly from behind the log-pile, start with the muzzles where you first | *expect to see the targets clearly against the sky, not as a blur against the undergrowth.*

Here the muzzles are too high so that you will either have to wait for the targets to rise above the gun before you can pick them up well—or there | *will be a tendency to intercept the target's line and stop the swing.*

if you pick up the target correctly the muzzles will be moving in an upward direction, along the target's flight line as well. If you cover up such a target with the muzzles you stand a good chance of shooting over its back. Exactly the same situation applies with a low oncoming target at, or about, eye-level, such as a driven grouse coming straight towards a butt. With these low on-comers the further out in front you take them, the more you need shoot at their legs. Contrary to what many people think, this feeling of shooting as the muzzles reach the bottom edge of the target often works well with 'springing teal' targets.

Medium oncoming pheasant
Gun brought into 'ready position' with muzzles
pointing safely towards top of cover as bird is first
seen.

For most right-handed shooters a target quartering in or quartering away on the left side needs little or no lead, always providing that you pick up the line properly from just behind and that the gun is kept moving as the shot is taken. The feeling will generally be one of shooting at the target as the muzzles move through.

With targets quartering in or away on the right side you will need to work a little harder to compensate for the unnatural swing. With all quartering shots be careful that you get the muzzles onto the line from just behind as it is very easy to intercept them and stop your swing.

Direct crossing shots will need a more conscious follow-through even when going from right to left (the natural swing). Direct crossing targets from left to right (that unnatural swing against the body) are

Front hand pushing out to pick up line of oncoming bird (from tail to beak) and to begin gun mounting action. Body weight forward on front foot.

normally the ones that need the greatest lead, the biggest gap between muzzle and target as the shot is made.

Medium oncoming targets need smoothly blocking out with the muzzles as the shot is made being careful not to stop the swing as the bird disappears from

view, whereas with really high on-comers you will need to bring your muzzles through and beyond the target in order to hit it.

Let me remind you again that these are all just guide-lines and that there is no

Medium oncoming pheasant (contd)
Body weight finishes still slightly forward, or fairly evenly balanced over both feet, depending on how far out in front bird can be safely shot. Gun is well up into cheek as muzzles blot out bird just before shot is taken.

substitute for some disciplined practice, a little repetition while you learn your own sight pictures for the various shots. As I've said before, providing you are doing the basic things correctly, do not be afraid of experiment. If you really are in trouble on

High pheasant overhead.
Gun brought into 'ready position' as bird is sighted, gun muzzles safely up above top of cover. On sloping ground with beaters often working above the guns extra care must be taken to avoid shooting into cover.

certain stands though, then take a lesson, preferably from someone you trust. In the long run it will be cheaper and far less frustrating than going on too long with the process of trial and error.

High pheasant overhead (contd.)

Front hand pushing forward to begin gun mount and pick up line of bird with muzzles. Weight well balanced over both feet.

High pheasant overhead (contd.)
*Do not start to mount the gun too soon, with any
bird that gives you a lot of time to look at it wait
until you feel you can make the shot in one smooth
movement.*

Gun mount completed just before bird is overtaken.
Front arm now nicely extended and body weight
coming back from waist on to back foot.

The Sesquicentennial set of guns commemorating the 150 years of Holland & Holland gun making in 1985, comprising a 10-bore muzzle-loading percussion gun, a 12-bore hammer gun and a 20-bore 'Royal'. The trio represent the three important periods in the history of gunmaking: the percussion era, the breech-loading hammer gun of the later 19th century and the culmination of the traditional skills passed on to today's craftsmen to produce the Holland and Holland 'Royal' of the 1990s.

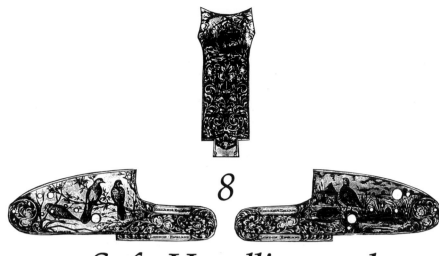

8

Safe Handling and Conduct in the Field

S HOTGUNS KILL. From the plain honest work horse through to the most exquisitely ornate, the basic function of a shotgun is to kill. This fact is one you must never forget, even those of you who have no intention of shooting at anything other than artificial targets; shotguns kill. At close range, even the smallest gauge gun is a quite fearsome weapon and so must be treated with the care and respect it deserves. Handling any weapon safely is largely a matter of common sense, though some users seem sadly lacking in this quality, usually simply through ignorance,

Patterns on a white-washed steel plate from a 12 bore gun, 1 oz No 7 shot through the ¼ choke barrel at 5, 10, 15, 20 and 25 yards. The circular cut-outs on the plate are 4″ in diameter.

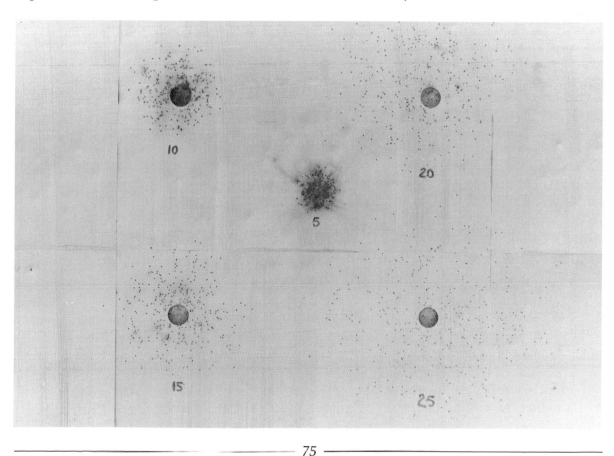

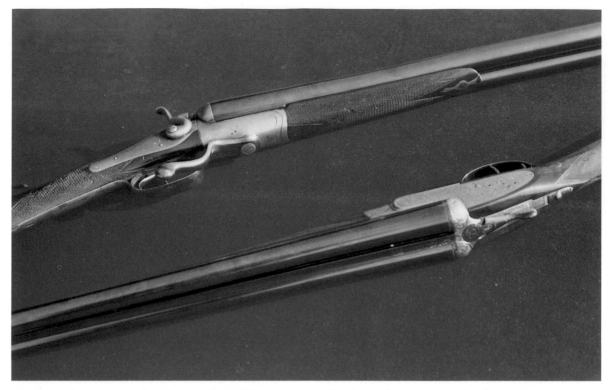

Two drop down action double-barrelled 12 bore shotguns. Lower gun with the familiar top lever opening. The older hammer-gun still in regular use has the more unusual under-lever opening.

never having been shown otherwise.

Ground rules

There are a number of ground rules which, if always obeyed, should keep the beginner out of serious trouble. After which, just as when using any weapon, tool or machinery competently, it is a matter of constant careful handling until its safe use becomes automatic, though never to the extent that over confidence might lead to carelessness.

Throughout this safety section I must assume that the guns you are using are in a safe condition for the job in hand, but if you are in any doubt about a gun's condition or the suitability of the ammunition you propose to use, then seek advice from a reputable gunsmith or dealer. Do not be afraid to ask, you may not get a second chance. For the newcomer 'proof-marks' on guns and the information, or lack of it, printed on cartridge boxes these days can be very confusing, especially now that a combination of both 'imperial' and 'metric' measurements are being used; so if you are in any doubt, find out.

Back to those ground rules: when picking up any closed gun, whether it is your own which *'you know is empty'*, or on taking any gun from a cover or rack, do so carefully. Do not touch the trigger(s), be absolutely certain that you do not point it towards anyone, and before doing anything else, *open the breech*. If you don't know how to open the gun to make it 'safe', then you have no right picking it up in the first place, so ask to be shown. This action of always opening a gun to check that it is empty and therefore 'safe' to handle takes but a moment, yet it takes only a moment for an accident to happen and you cannot bring back a charge of shot once you've sent it on its way. Make this action a habit as soon as you pick up any closed gun. Before doing anything else, open it to check that it is empty. Almost all double-barrelled guns open by pushing across the top-lever and privoting down the barrels on their hinge, in order to expose the chambers. Just occasionally, on some older side-by-side guns, you might come across one with side lever or under lever opening, but the drop down action of the barrels is just the same once the lever is activated.

Single-barrelled guns of the 'pump-action' or 'semi-automatic' variety should be treated with extra care as the breech

Carrying 'pump-action' or 'semi-automatic', shotguns safely between stands. Muzzles up and action slides open to show clear chambers.

cannot be opened by dropping down the barrel, so the action slides of these guns must be kept open to show an empty chamber when carried, uncovered, between stands. Though these guns are not normally used here in the game field, under careful supervision a semi-automatic shotgun can be very useful in starting off any youngster or lady who is 'recoil-shy'; much of the energy, which would otherwise produce felt recoil as the gun is fired, is used up in the working action of the gun. Apart from being able to see straight away whether or not a gun is loaded by dropping down the barrels, the other big advantage with any drop down action is that you can look straight through the tubes from the breech end to make certain that they are clear of any obstruction before loading the gun. Anything found in the barrels (and it can be something left after the last cleaning which shouldn't happen but it does; or something picked up as the gun is slipped into its cover; or material such as mud or snow entering the muzzles if the gun is carried carelessly or dropped) must be removed completely before the gun is

loaded. Never ever try to shoot out a blockage, no matter how slight; at best you will bulge the gun barrel; at worst you will burst the barrel with horrifying results.

The wrong cartridge
The classic cause of a burst barrel, sometimes with fatal results, is a 20 bore cartridge lodged in a 12 bore gun. Now you might think that that cannot happen, but believe me it is all too easy to do. Let me set the scene for you. A father accompanies his son or daughter out shooting. The youngster is using a 20 bore gun. Father is not shooting. He's looking after his offspring, keeping an eye on things from a safety point of view, offering some guidance and helpfully carrying a pocketful of the youngster's 20 bore cartridges. At the end of the day he empties his pocket of cartridges, or so he thinks, hangs up his shooting jacket, not knowing that lurking in a corner of that spacious pocket is a time bomb; he's missed one!

A week later it is father's turn to shoot, a good day out at driven pheasants. He's arrived at the appointed place in good time and begins to make ready as the other guns gather. He assembles his gun, slides it carefully into the gun-slip, tops up his cartridge bag, and for good measure he

Looking through the tubes from the breech to make certain they are clear of any obstruction before loading.

empties a box of his 12 bore cartridges into that same spacious pocket. The time bomb is ticking.

Not much to shoot at on the first drive. He's drawn an end peg to start the day. The second drive is better though and he's shooting quite well. Anticipation rises as he arrives at his peg for the third. He knows this drive well and he's in 'the pound seat'. A quick look through the gun after taking it from the slip; all clear, so he loads from his pocket and waits for the first bird to break cover. A couple of minutes later and here it comes, a good high hen, rising and curling, heading straight towards him, but he's too eager after the waiting and misses it with both barrels, then to make matters worse old so-and-so on the next peg deals with it cleanly behind the line. 'Nice shot' he acknowledges through clenched teeth as he reloads, giving the cartridges in his pocket a good shake to make them easier to get at—and it's ticking more loudly. Five minutes later with the drive well under way he's feeling

much better. He's had a steady trickle of birds over and got well into his swing. He's just thinking about topping up his pocket from the cartridge bag when there's a sudden flush of birds from the covert. He kills one with his second shot, dives into his pocket for cartridges while still keeping an eye on the birds coming towards the line, and into the left barrel goes the time bomb, dropping through the chamber and lodging firmly at the lead in from chamber to barrel, but there's too much going on to hear the ticking. He shoots a bird with his right barrel just as another dozen or so pheasants flush through the tops of the trees and head towards him. Watching them he quickly opens the gun, grabs a handful of cartridges from his bag on the ground and puts them into his pocket. The ticking is deafening. Looking down briefly he reloads both barrels, the 12 bore cartridge in the left chamber sits neatly on top of the 20 bore cartridge. As he closes the gun he has already picked the birds he hopes will be his first right and left of the

Loading the gun with muzzles pointing towards the ground.

In the past we were always told to close the gun by bringing the stock up to the barrels, all very well if the gun closes easily . . .

not so good if the gun is stiff to close especially for a youngster or lady who may well finish up by closing the gun dangerously close to their own feet.

Turn the gun over slightly and lock the stock between your side and arm . . . Slide your front hand down the barrel for a little more leverage.

Lean forward over the gun as you push up with the front hand, closing at the ground 3 or 4 feet in front.

Definitely not the way to close a gun. Remember that a gun can go off as you close it. Where will the shot finish up if this gun goes off as I close it?

When game shooting, having loaded the gun, keep the muzzles pointing safely skywards.

With clay targets after loading the gun, come into the 'ready' position, with your muzzles at the point you wish to pick up the target's line—as in this unusual sporting clays situation.

Waiting, gun in safe relaxed position. Safety catch in 'safe' position.

Up into the 'ready' position, the catch is pushed off 'safe', finger on trigger-guard, thumb curled over grip of stock.

Gun fully mounted, finger on trigger, thumb well clear of safety catch, no risk of a split thumb on the top-lever.

day. The first bird folds up neatly and as he swings through the second he's thinking, 'This is just like that first bird I missed. Old so-and-so next door is not having this one.' The bomb goes off.

Although the combination is much more unlikely, a similar situation can occur with a 28 bore cartridge in a 16 bore gun, though this time the 28 bore cartridge will probably lodge at the choke cone.

There was a time when all 12 bore cartridges were red, all 16 bores blue and all 20 bores yellow, a simple colour coding which worked well. Those days are long gone so that now all bore sizes seem to be available in any colour under the sun.

The lesson is very simple: keep cartridges of different bore sizes separate, and make absolutely certain that you empty your pockets or bag completely after using a different cartridge from normal. So before putting in the first cartridge(s) at the beginning of a drive or at each new stand look briefly through the open gun to check that all is clear before loading. Make this a

Don't stand next to this guy! Not a safe waiting position.

This waiting position is very 'border-line'. Trigger guard uppermost and muzzles pointing upwards is fine until the arm becomes tired when the muzzles become lower and lower.

habit also if you stumble with or drop the gun or if you fire a shot that sounds or feels different from normal. On opening the gun, eject or take out the cartridges, blow into the chambers to clear any smoke and check for any obstruction before re-loading.

I recently had a father bring his eleven-year-old son to the school for his first lesson. The gun produced was a double-barrelled .410 carried in a full length cover. The gun was taken from the cover, opened and carried in the approved way, over the forearm, to our 'fitting plates' where I began by going through the safety rules. On looking through the gun I found I could not see through either barrel. A suitable rod was produced and two 3" plugs of drying mud emerged, one from each muzzle. On enquiring how the gun had got into this condition, the youngster said that his older brother had dropped it in a muddy field while out shooting the previous weekend!! Father got the rocket.

Muzzles up!
Now, having opened the gun and checked that the barrels are clear and safe to load,

the next step is to keep the muzzles pointing safely towards the ground three or four feet ahead of yourself throughout the loading and closing operation. In the past we were always told to close a gun by bringing the stock up to the barrels, never by bringing the barrels up to the stock, simply in order to keep the muzzles pointing towards the ground. This is fair enough with any gun that opens and closes easily, but many new cheaper guns can be extremely stiff to close especially for a youngster or lady, and if they endeavour to do so by bringing the stock up to the barrels in the manner prescribed, they often finish up covering their own feet. In such a situation, once the cartridges are in the chambers, hold the gun firmly in both hands, turn the gun over slightly to the right and lock the stock between your side and your right arm. Slide your left hand down the barrels to gain a little more leverage and lean forward over the gun as you push up with the left hand. This should result in you being able to close the gun and still keep the muzzles pointing

One of the interesting characters employed in pheasant shooting and worth listening to.

safely towards the ground. Once the gun is closed, if you are game shooting, then either keep the muzzles pointing safely at the ground, or better still safely skywards, until a target presents itself. If shooting clay targets, then after closing the gun bring it into the 'ready position' before calling for your target.

The safety catch

Up until now I have quite purposely not mentioned 'the safety catch', one of the biggest misnomers ever. No safety catch ever made a gun 'safe'. All it really does is stop you from pulling the trigger accidentally. A gun can go off as you close it, whether the safety catch is applied or not. Once a gun is loaded and closed, the action is fully cocked and just waiting to go off. I am still amazed sometimes by someone who perhaps fails to get off a shot through having forgotten to push the catch forwards, saying 'I didn't cock the gun'. The safety catch has nothing to do with the action of cocking the gun. Let me say again: the safety catch simply stops you from pulling the trigger accidentally; any closed gun, with or without the safety catch

applied, must be treated as being loaded and liable to go off. The only safe gun is the one with the breech open and empty.

There are basically two types of safety catch found on modern shotguns, usually termed 'automatic' and 'non-automatic' or 'manual'. The 'automatic' catch is the one found on most guns built for game shooting, 'automatic' simply because on opening the gun after firing a shot, the action of pushing over the top-lever also pushes the catch back into the 'safe' position. Thus the catch must be pushed off 'safe' again each time the gun is reloaded in order to fire the next two shots. The non-automatic or manual catch on the other hand, once pushed off 'safe', stays in that mode until you yourself pull it back to the 'safe' position. This manual catch is normally found on guns built for competition work and, as in competition you will not load the gun until you are on the stand ready to shoot, once the catch is pushed 'off' there can be no chance of losing a target through forgetting the 'safety catch', no matter how many times you open and close the gun. Indeed some guns used in competition will have the catch de-activated and fixed in the 'off' position or even done away with altogether, and providing such guns are used for the purpose for which they are designed there is nothing wrong with this practice.

In the past it has been recommended that, when using a gun equipped with an 'automatic' safety catch while game shooting, the catch be pushed 'off' as the gun was mounted. To my mind this is not good practice, firstly because you must not trust the catch to make the gun 'safe' and secondly because I have seen too many people injure themselves (usually by splitting open the top of the right thumb on the gun's top-lever) while trying to push the catch 'off' during the mounting of the gun or with one finger already on the trigger. The result is inevitable: a slightly premature discharge before the gun is fully mounted. The thumb pushing the catch forward is right behind the top-lever and the result is a painful and bloody injury, particularly if hands are cold or wet as they

'Picker-up', often waiting unobtrusively under a tree or against a hedge with his/her dogs.

often are when game shooting in our fickle climate. Far better to take off the catch before you mount the gun, and the 'ready position' gives the ideal opportunity to do this safely. You will only come into the 'ready position' when a shot seems imminent, so this is the time to take off the catch, long before you should have a finger near the triggers. If the expected shot does not materialize, then you will not keep the gun in the 'ready position', so back comes the catch to 'safe', and down comes the gun into a more relaxed waiting position until the next opportunity arises.

It didn't go off!

If at any time while game or clay target shooting a gun fails to fire as you attempt to shoot, and it can be for any number of reasons—cold, wet hands, forgetting the safety catch, too heavy a trigger pull (ideally a good crisp pull of 3½/4 lbs suits most people), not releasing a single-trigger cleanly after firing the first shot etc—don't stand there playing with the trigger saying, 'Look, it didn't go off!' Take your finger from the trigger, keep the gun pointing safely at the ground and open it. If the gun fails to fire a second time then have it checked over by a good gunsmith. One of the worst frights I have ever had happened many years ago when I had gone to coach

at a skeet club in Scandinavia. It was on my first day there with the first pupil, a man who should have known better. He chose to begin on Station 2 on the skeet field. After going through the preliminaries he loaded two cartridges in the under-and-over gun he was using, took up his starting position for a single high house bird and the next few seconds I will never forget. I can still see every detail vividly in slow motion. He called for the target, mounted the gun on it but the gun failed to fire. In a continuation of the same turn he was making to take the shot, he brought the gun off his shoulder with the gun pointing at waist level. Finger still on the trigger, he turned to face me and before I could move I had the muzzles of a fully-loaded gun pointing straight at my ribs from a distance of about 6" with its holder saying, 'It didn't go off.' The sick feeling in my stomach was one I hope you never experience and I know what it feels like to become 'rooted to the spot'. I didn't dare move or shout, but somehow managed to remain at least outwardly calm and quietly asked him to take his finger from the trigger and turn away. By this time there was a look of horror on his face also, as he realised what he had done. The gun functioned perfectly for the rest of the lesson, though for some reason I don't think either of us gave of our best. It was a salutary lesson on both sides, so remember: an accident takes but a second to happen and I thought I was

When standing out on rough plough, providing it is not frozen solid, stamp out a flat patch on which to stand.

standing in a safe position.

Getting used to your gun
After receiving some initial instruction in safe gun handling, it used to be common practice for the budding shot to spend a season or two out in the shooting field armed with an empty gun.

During this time he was expected to carry and handle the gun as though it was loaded, to act in fact as one of the party, while his actions were monitored by his seniors. Any unsafe behaviour would be quickly jumped on and corrected until the youngster was judged safe and responsible enough to be given charge of a loaded gun, though still under supervision for a probationary period until he proved safe enough to be left on his own. These outings may have been full days at driven game, a simple foray out for a couple of rabbits, a morning or evening spent on a marsh or fore-shore, some pigeon decoying, a winter's afternoon at wood pigeon coming to roost, a chance to walk a snipe bog or a day out ferreting. Every experience was invaluable at an age when lessons learned usually left life-long impressions. Apart from learning how to handle a gun safely and politely, much knowledge was gained

Even the best run shoots will occasionally produce some low birds.

as to what went into making a shooting day, and a great deal was learned about the countryside in general such as bird and mammal recognition and learning to read the many signs left by the same. The identification of trees, wild flowers, grasses, insects and so on, along with field-craft and folk-lore, passed on, perhaps, to an inquisitive young mind by any one of the interesting characters employed or living in and around the rural scene, could kindle an ongoing interest in and a deep-seated love for natural history. There is so much more to a day out with a gun than just the shooting. A seemingly ordinary outing can be transformed suddenly and unexpectedly by the sight or discovery of something new or unusual, or a blank evening on a marsh made memorable by a spectacular sky or rare bird.

Sadly these days fewer and fewer youngsters get the opportunity or go through such an important formative period. With dwindling numbers of people working on the land and in the countryside

as a whole, but with more and more people gaining access to it, field sports, the very activities which for so long have helped form the overall country scene in so many places, seem to be constantly under threat. Any youngster expressing an interest should be encouraged and if possible taken under someone's wing for a period, while being shown the right way to do things, and how to behave well in the countryside.

Having learned to load, close and otherwise handle a gun safely, the problem on each stand when shooting at clay targets for practice or pleasure at a responsibly organised ground is purely one of working out how best to deal successfully with each target presented. Now that might sound rather obvious, but in such a situation, with the possible exception of properly protected trap operators, there will be no-one in the shooting areas to worry about, so that you can concentrate on the targets without having to be concerned with what is behind them, knowing that your shot is going into a safe area.

In the field

As a beginner shooting live game, you will

One very basic and important rule when dealing with driven pheasants: never shoot at any bird unless it clearly has sky behind it.

face many more safety problems, and here one of the most important is the background against which you shoot. The golden rule must be never to shoot where you cannot see where your shot will finish up. If you are fortunate enough to have the opportunity to shoot at driven birds—and for most beginners that will mean driven pheasants—then firstly listen carefully to any instructions given at the beginning of the day by your host, shoot captain or head-keeper. Apart from telling you what form the day will take, and how you will be expected to move around the numbered pegs on each drive, you will be given specific instructions as to what you may or may not shoot, and one of the most usual instructions given during this pre-shoot briefing on a driven pheasant day is 'No ground game'. To all intents and purposes this means no shooting at rabbits or hares, though with more deer than ever about now, roe and muntjac are often seen during a drive, but must not be taken with a shotgun. Foxes coming through the

shooting line should also be left alone, though specific instructions are sometimes given, on certain drives, that they may be shot. As a beginner, *don't do it*. Not only can such shots be very risky unless you know the ground well and can remain calm, but to be as certain as you can be of killing a fox cleanly with a standard load of No.6 or 7 shot, you should not be shooting at one beyond fifteen yards. Remember that the reason you are standing in line as part of a team of guns is to shoot driven pheasants. The reasons for this instruction, 'No ground game', should be fairly clear even to the beginner. Other than the team of eight or so guns, often with companions and dogs, there will be quite a number of people within gun-shot range,* the most obvious being the line of beaters normally getting closer to the guns as each drive progresses. Less obvious may be a keeper or beater acting as a 'stop' in a ditch or hedgerow to prevent birds running rather than flying from cover, while some distance behind the shooting line, usually waiting unobtrusively under a tree or against a hedge, will be various 'pickers-up' with their dogs, ready to do their work at the end of the drive. All of the afore-mentioned are at risk from low shots.

The shooting line

Having reached your allotted peg for the start of a drive, the first thing to do is to have a look around to ascertain where you can and perhaps more importantly, where you cannot safely shoot. If the pegs marking each gun's position are out in the open and in a reasonably straight line, then you can normally see quite easily where the other guns are standing, but life isn't always that simple. Your immediate neighbours may be concealed from you by trees, hedgerows, sloping ground and so on, or you may well find that you are placed

*Remember that although a shotgun is looked upon as a short-range weapon and that your maximum effective range on live quarry is about fifty yards, depending on the angle at which the shot is taken and the size of the pellets used, your shot can travel a couple of hundred yards. At this distance the shot will be falling harmlessly, but at over a hundred yards individual pellets will have enough energy to pierce an eye and can blind.

in a clearing in a wood, or on a ride or fire-break so that even though the guns on either side of you may be no more than forty yards away, you can see nothing of them. So make certain you know where they are before the drive begins, and just as important, let them know where you are—often all it takes is a little whistle or call and an acknowledging wave. A further complication may well be that the guns are not set out in a straight line. They may well form an **L** or **U** shape along two or three sides of a covert or sometimes be double-banked with perhaps five or six guns in the front line and the others forming a second rank some distance behind. This may well make for some challenging shooting but extra care must be taken if you find yourself in the back row.

Once on your peg, unless given specific instructions to do otherwise, you should not leave it until the drive is over. At the start of the drive, having had a good look around to be certain that you know where everyone is, check and load the gun safely and wait in as relaxed but alert a manner as possible, preferably with your gun muzzles

Beaters working down this Yorkshire hillside could be in danger from any shot not taken against the sky.

pointing up rather than down, especially once the drive gets going, so that at no stage do you have to bring your gun through the beating line.

When has a drive started?

Whereas it is normally quite clear that a drive is over—with the keeper blowing a long whistle or horn blast to signal an end to the shooting as or before beaters reach the edge of the covert or crop they have worked through; or indeed by beaters walking up to or through the line of butts to complete a grouse drive—it may not always be obvious that a drive has started. This should not be a problem when shooting driven grouse as once the line is out and you are settled in your butt, having decided where you can and cannot safely shoot, you should be ready for action at any time, though it is more than likely that a good fifteen minutes or more will elapse before the first birds appear.

On other occasions, as when starting the shooting day with a duck drive or when dealing with wild partridges for example, very precise instructions may be given (and should be listened to carefully), as to how the operation will proceed.—Not to slam vehicle doors, to approach your peg carefully and quietly, not to talk as you walk to your shooting position and not to shoot at anything before the signal to start is given.

Doubt as to whether or not a drive is in fact under way can occur with pheasants. Birds may be in the air before you reach your peg, usually as a result of being pushed from patches of cover into the main body of the drive by beaters 'blanking in'. No matter how tempting, the rule 'no shooting between drives' must be strictly obeyed. The only time this rule may be broken is if you are requested by the keeper, host or shoot captain to dispatch a wounded bird which is sitting beyond reach in a tree. If you are requested to do this remember that a shotgun normally shoots a little high. There is nothing more embarrassing than missing a sitting target at twenty yards by shooting harmlessly over its back while others are watching. So try not to get too close and sit the bird just on top of your muzzles as you shoot. Having reached your peg and having made the usual safety checks, unless you have been told to wait for a specific signal, then you should consider the drive to be under way and be prepared to shoot.

Pay some attention to your feet; a good stance goes without saying, but you need as level a base as possible to give of your best. Stood out on a rough plough, providing it isn't frozen solid, it is easy enough to make yourself a flat patch. In woodland kick away any twigs and stones from under your feet.

In hilly countryside, hopefully your host will have made certain that there is a levelled patch at each peg, there are enough safety problems to deal with without having to be an acrobat to boot. Some of our older game shooters are not the fittest and most agile, and no-one needs the added problems of fighting to keep their balance each time a shot is fired. Think twice before going back to such a shoot.

Occasionally a drive may be 'taken away from the guns', that is the beaters will be walking away from the shooting line with

Grouse butts on a Scottish moor, often not more than fifty yards apart, but you can easily become isolated in a sea of heather.

birds flushing ahead of them and, because of the lie of the land or the way the wind is blowing on the day, the birds will break back over the beating line towards the guns, offering far better shooting than might be had if the birds were pushed directly to the guns in the conventional manner. More often than not though, beaters will be closing with the line of guns or moving across your front, so that no shots must be taken into the trees where beaters are. This is particularly important if the ground is sloping down towards the guns, where, in some parts of the country often notable for high birds, the beaters may be well above you, so that some shots you might safely take on flatter ground now become unsafe.

Low birds

Even the best run shoots will occasionally produce some low birds, perhaps through a sudden change in wind strength or direction or because a day is particularly still and bright. No bird will fly well against the sun and it is for this reason that you may find yourself squinting against a low winter's sun all day long and not because your host or keeper has a twisted sense of humour, so take along a pair of dark glasses. Low birds are potentially more dangerous than ground game, especially when passing in front of the guns where shots taken would almost be bound to go into cover where beaters are working, or when passing between you and a neighbouring gun when any shot would endanger others in the shooting line. Woodcock flushing with pheasants from cover may encourage you to fire potentially dangerous shots as they twist and turn through the trees and must be treated with extra care no matter how tempting the prize. Towards the end of the season you may be encouraged to shoot cock birds that have passed through the line too low to be shot at safely in front and they certainly must not be shot at over your neighbour's head. Such birds, though can make quite testing targets once safely behind your neighbour, always providing that you turn correctly through the shooting line with the gun off your

Once in this sunken butt, the marker sticks are an absolute must. (Photo taken while making game shooting video.)

shoulder and the muzzles pointing upwards and that you know where the pickers-up are waiting—but these are not shots for a beginner to take on without practice or supervision. For the beginner the best thing to do with low birds is to ignore them as far as firing a shot goes and leave them for another day. You should not even think about raising your gun at them. Keep it in a safe waiting (not 'ready') position, preferably with the muzzles pointing upwards; don't wave your arms or gun or anything else at low birds coming through the line in an effort to make them gain height, a dangerous practice which will not make the bird go any higher and can only serve to make you look rather silly.

With so many things to consider, any newcomer to driven pheasant shooting can be forgiven for feeling more than a little apprehensive on the first few outings or for feeling somewhat overawed by the occasion and afraid of doing anything wrong. All these feelings are quite natural when first doing anything new, if you are in any doubt about taking a shot, then DON'T. No-one will mind you being over-cautious to begin with. Far better to leave the field at the end of the day, having perhaps let a few more birds than necessary go by not shot at, than to shoot

brilliantly but having taken one dangerous shot. In the first instance, you will be welcomed back, in the second, no-one will want to know you.

Walking gun

When shooting driven pheasants there is one other duty you may be asked to perform, that of being a 'walking gun'. On some shoots there are just certain drives where this happens, others will call for a walking gun on most drives where it becomes almost an automatic duty for the gun who at that time is drawn at one or other of the end pegs in the shooting line. As well as an opportunity to be on the move with the beaters instead of standing still freezing at a peg on a cold day, this posting is often one to look forward to as it can offer some unusual and testing shots. You must take extra care to be safe though, as you will be on the move, sometimes over rough ground and through thick cover, with a number of beaters close to you. You may be asked to walk for the whole of the drive or for only part of it until you reach your numbered peg where you then remain until the drive is completed. You may be walking just ahead of, level with or just behind the end of the beating line, or walking behind the beaters somewhere towards the middle of the line. Your duty as walking gun is not to shoot at birds which are flushed and fly forward towards

You have to take shots well out in front at birds flying at or below eye-level.

Grouse appearing low over the heather looking like nothing less than a squadron of jet fighters.

the main shooting line (when you would of course be shooting at the waiting guns anyway!) but to try and deal with those birds which flush back over the beaters' heads or slip out sideways from the drive. As you walk keep the gun pointing safely skywards all the while—open and unload it if you have to cross any awkward obstacle. If you are walking behind the beaters you may be presented with some shots curling back over you, very much like a normal driven bird, but more often than not you will have to turn to shoot behind the beating line as birds break back. As you turn through the beaters you must keep your muzzles up and the stock out of your shoulder in just the same way as you would make a safe turn to shoot behind a neighbouring gun when standing in the shooting line. Birds breaking out sideways must also be treated with care as, though they may offer testing crossing shots, they may not get up particularly high, so be careful about the background you are shooting towards. There is one very basic, but very important rule when shooting at driven pheasants and that is never to shoot at any bird unless it clearly has sky behind it.

Partridges

This same rule should also be applied to partridges. There was a time when driven partridge shooting meant good coveys of our native grey birds exploding over high hedge tops or appearing suddenly over and through belts of trees to challenge the waiting guns, offering a mixture of the problems found with driven pheasants and grouse. These days, with the decline of the grey partridge and the disappearance of many hedgerows and tree belts, driven partridge shooting, more often than not, means the reared red-legged bird, pushed over the guns from downland hill tops or over valleys in much the same way as pheasants, when perhaps the biggest problem for the gun is one of picking out individual birds from large groups going over the shooting line.

The grouse butt

Driven grouse can offer some of the most exciting and challenging bird shooting in the United Kingdom. Red grouse numbers fluctuate enormously from year to year even on the best moors, but, given a season with a reasonable number of birds, anyone

Driven grouse sequence—low oncoming birds.
As covey appears low on horizon, gun comes into 'ready position' with muzzles down just below line of chosen oncoming bird.

Front hand pushing forward to pick up bird's line from underneath, body weight moving forward over front foot.

Gun mount completed with stock well up into cheek as muzzles 'touch' bird's bottom edge. Body weight well forward on front foot; the weight is really following the front hand as it pushes the gun forward towards the bird during the gun mount. Low oncoming birds shot at well out in front are very easy to miss by shooting over their backs. Having picked up the bird's line with the muzzles, keep the bird on top of the muzzles as the shot is taken. The feeling is often one of shooting at the legs of the bird.

Good waiting position for most of the drive—muzzles low over front of butt so that no matter how low birds appear you can pick up their line as soon as you see them.

In contrast—muzzles too high while waiting, making it difficult to pick up line of low birds. This position will make for bad gun mounting and late shots.

After the signal that the beaters are nearing the end of the drive and that no more shots must be taken in front of the butts. This position is safe for beaters and allows a turn with the muzzles kept pointing upwards, stock down out of the shoulder, for any birds which are shot at behind the butts towards the end of a drive.

Never prop a gun up like this, loaded or not, especially in a hide or grouse butt, or with dogs about. A broken stock or damaged barrels are costly to repair or replace.

in a position to try this unique shooting experience should take it. There is no other shooting quite like it. There may be a few still, hot days in late August or early September, especially in a year with a large number of late young birds, when their shooting seems almost easy, but the air is rarely still for long on those heather-covered hillsides. Once these birds are strong on the wing and with the onset of cooler, wilder weather, September and October grouse will test the best of shots.

From the very way they fly, the nature of the ground over which they fly and the way in which the butts are sited, the most likely place for a game shooting 'accident' has to be in a line of butts when shooting at driven grouse. Here the experienced gun can be as guilty as the beginner of firing a dangerous shot, perhaps even more so through becoming slightly careless or over-confident and cutting down the safe angles on either side of the butt in an effort to take

an extra bird from a covey. Sometimes the older man, having shot well and safely for many years, suddenly finds that, through advancing age, eyesight and reactions are not what they used to be and that birds flying against the heather become more and more difficult to see, especially in bad light and rain. Under such conditions, late and therefore potentially dangerous shots become almost inevitable. Hopefully most people will realize or be told in time what is beginning to happen and do something about it before doing anything they may regret.

On the other hand anyone shooting at driven grouse for the first time is likely to be so wary of making a dangerous shot that they will quite rightly tend to err on the side of caution and forego some shots they might otherwise safely take. A dangerous shot on a grouse moor can range from peppering a beater at a hundred yards or more which, though no less forgivable, may do nothing more than raise a fist or a few choice words providing the recipient is not hit in the face, to placing a shot directly into the next butt at forty or fifty yards with very serious injury to its occupant(s).

If as a beginner going into a butt for the first time you really are afraid of making a mistake (a natural enough fear for most people), then try loading just one barrel of the gun so that you will not be tempted to fire a late second shot or make up your mind to shoot only at birds well out in front of the butts and not to turn around and shoot behind the line until you gain more confidence. Both these exercises will give you one thing less to worry about and enable you to watch some birds fly to and through the line and so learn something about the way they behave.

Preparing for the drive
Once in your butt, the first thing to do as you prepare for the drive, even before you take your gun from its cover, is to make absolutely certain that you know which way the shooting line runs and where your neighbouring butts are. Obvious as this may sound, due to its sloping nature and the undulations in the ground you will be

The seasoned grouse shooter in this well-constructed butt is relaxed and waiting quietly on his shooting seat. Note the dark glasses worn against the low sun. No sticks at the top of the butt though the gun slip has been strategically placed on one side.

shooting over, even though the butts are normally not more than fifty yards apart, you may be able to see none of them and find that you appear to be completely isolated in a sea of heather. In such a situation you should find that the position of the next butts is marked by posts in the ground, hopefully painted white, to show you which way the line runs, and that if you look carefully, even though you cannot see the butt, you may just see your neighbour's head above the heather. These days, most butts will have a couple of moveable marker sticks in them or you may be given a pair at the start of the day to carry with you. Though these sticks cannot physically stop you from swinging your gun dangerously through the line of butts (only you can do that), use them to define the limits of your safe shooting arc in front of your butt, and not just to mark the position of your neighbour. If you do that and swing as far as the stick, your gun will be pointing down the line. Ideally four such sticks should be supplied, so that you can mark out the same angles behind you, demarcating a definite 'no go' area, but two

is all you will get in most situations. Butts vary enormously in height and shape and in the materials used for their construction. Ideally you should be able to stand fairly well forward and use the front of the butt, which is normally turfed or heather covered, as a shelf on which to lean and help support the weight of your gun once the drive is under way. So, having made sure you know where your neighbours are, decide how far forward or back you will stand to shoot. The main deciding factors here will be the height of the front of the butt, your own height and whether or not you can then open and close your gun over the front of the butt to reload or whether you have to open and close it inside the butt itself. If the latter, be very careful, especially in stone-built butts, that you don't dent your gun barrels against the stone-work. If you now look straight ahead in the direction from which the drive is being brought (in other words, at right angles from the line of butts), you should be able to give yourself an angle of about 45° on either side of this line and thus open up an angle of about 90° in which it will be

Grouse over the butt.

safe for you to shoot until you get the signal that it is no longer safe to shoot in front, as the beaters are about to appear in front of you. There is a similar angle behind the line where you can shoot at birds which have gone through the butts. Whenever you are in one of the end butts of the line then these angles will change on one side as you will usually have the presence of a flanker to contend with. The success or failure of a drive can hinge on skillful flanking to turn birds which would otherwise break out to the side, back towards the guns. A flanker may already be in position as you get to the end butt, in which case he will be standing up to let you know where he is, give him an acknowledging wave as you place your marker stick in the top of the butt to show his position; or he will go out to his position once you are in your butt, when you can acknowledge his position and mark it in the same way. Once the drive begins the flanker will often be crouched in the heather watching the progress of the drive carefully, only showing himself or his flag, at the moment he chooses best to turn birds to the line, so that for most of the

drive you will not normally be able to see him. This will mean that you effectively cut down your shooting arc in front, but at the same time open up a shooting area on your left or right side, depending on which end of the line you are.

Judging distances

Having decided where you can and cannot shoot—and just in case you are not supplied with marker sticks for some reason, remember that you can always improvise by using perhaps your gun-slip on one side and your cartridge bag on the other—your next problem is going to be one of judging distance. In some butts this is not a problem; because of the way your butt is positioned your horizon may be only 30 or 40 yards away in front so that as soon as birds appear you will know that they are in range. In other butts you may find that you have 150 yards or so before the ground falls away behind a slope and that there will be hollows or gulleys in front of you where birds can suddenly disappear and reappear as they closely follow the contours of the ground. With no hedgerows or trees to relate to, just thousands of acres of rolling heather, give or take the occasional stone wall or fence-line, it becomes notoriously difficult to judge just how far away birds might be. In such a situation what you need to try and do is estimate a distance of at least 50 yards directly in front of your butt, then try and relate it to a sport you are familiar with, the length of a cricket-pitch, tennis court, a particular golf-shot, any sort of distance that you are used to judging along the ground. Having made your estimate, try and pick out some mark at that distance, a rock perhaps, a change in the heather height or colour, a patch of bracken; you should be able to find some feature on the ground that will help. (Oh, for a kindly keeper with an armful of whites pegs willing to put one in the ground at fifty yards in front of each butt wherever possible.) If you now join up your fifty yards estimate in an arc to meet the sides of your approximate 90° safe shooting angle you should now have a fairly clearly delineated area in which you should be starting to shoot as soon as birds appear. Now you may feel that 50 yards is a long way off (actually 60 yards after some experience is perhaps even better), but remember this: most of the birds that come through will be flying straight towards the line and, even at a modest 30 m.p.h., they will travel about 15 yards in one second. With a strong tail wind they may be going at twice that speed so that even if you force yourself to start at 60 yards, by the time you've picked one, or hopefully two, birds

This gun was unloaded, but how often do you see a trusting dog in this position?

from a covey as they constantly change position, looking like nothing less than a squadron of jet fighters coming at you, they are through the line and gone.

Shooting grouse is difficult

If your previous experience of driven bird shooting has been only at pheasants, you will probably have realized by now that what you have to do in order to kill grouse safely out in front of the butts is almost the opposite to that which you have got used to doing in order to shoot pheasants safely. With the pheasants, particularly with good birds coming off a hillside to guns in the valley below, if you start to shoot too soon you may be firing at birds which are out of shot or else shooting into the cover on the hillside in front of you, so endangering the beaters. Remember the rule always to have clear sky behind every bird. Try and do that with grouse and in some situations you will not fire a shot. You have to take shots well out in front at birds flying to or across you often below eye-level and below the sky-line; you are virtually being invited to shoot at ground game! This then is why the butts are sited to keep some higher ground between you and the beaters for most of the drive, so that no matter how low birds are when they approach the butts they are safe to shoot at for most of the drive, inside the safe arc you have given yourself. Though you may see the beaters or their flags waving on a hillside half a mile or more away at the beginning of the drive, you will then not see them again until the drive is almost over. They will be working their way towards you protected from your shots by the lie of the land. Only as they approach the last ridge before the line of butts will you get the signal that you must no longer shoot in front. The signal is normally a long blast on a horn and as they come over the last ridge they will hold their flags high above their heads. So on hearing the horn, or on seeing a flag appear above the sky-line, you must bring your gun up from its low waiting position on the front of the butt (the correct starting position to approach low birds), to point your muzzles vertically in the air. Any birds flushed after the horn has blown must not be shot at in

This is a safe shooting area but shot can ricochet from water.

front, no matter how tempting, but must be turned safely on with your muzzles still pointing skyward, to be shot at safely behind the butts. Once the drive is over, carefully unload your gun, check it again before putting it back in its cover. Then help to pick up any birds you have downed and hopefully marked, in the heather.

Waiting for the grouse

One final point on grouse, though not one strictly concerning safety, may help you avoid using up a great deal of nervous energy and becoming so tense that you jump to attention on the appearance of anything in your fore-ground, be it a grouse, a pipit, a bumble-bee or even a midge. Once settled in your butt there may be a wait of 15 to 20 minutes before anything much happens. Sometimes a few early birds may appear, probably flushed by a flanker moving into position, but there is normally a long wait before the first coveys reach the line. Try not to use up too much nervous energy straining your eyes by constantly scanning the ground in front. Rather try to relax, sit back on your shooting stick if you are using one, or just lean quietly on the front or side of the butt. If the top of the butt front forms a good flat

shelf, there is nothing wrong with laying the gun down flat for a while, always providing you keep the muzzles pointing safely forwards and you are certain that the gun cannot slide off. Never stand the loaded gun upright inside the butt, as that is just asking for trouble. Don't try and hide yourself completely in the butt—if you crouch down too low you won't see much and the movement you cause by bobbing up and down to try and see what is going on is far more likely to turn birds away from the butts than if you just stand normally and keep still until you need to mount your gun. Try not to get too tense as you wait; the chances of the first covey coming to your butt are one in eight so you are much more likely to be warned of approaching birds by hearing shots somewhere else along the line or a low whistle from the next butt.

Rough shooting

So far I have concentrated largely on safe gun handling in driven bird situations, simply because if you are fortunate enough to start your shooting career with driven birds, there will be comparatively large numbers of people around you on such days, all of whom are in potential danger from a carelessly fired shot. For most beginners, though, organised driven bird shooting will seem a million miles away,

When lined out in the open it is easy to see where your neighbouring guns are.

with first opportunities at live quarry much more likely to be some form of walking up, flighting, decoying or any one of the other activities loosely covered by the blanket term 'rough shooting'. It is during outings such as these, though, that you will learn a great deal of fieldcraft, much about your hoped-for quarry and about the countryside itself, especially when fortunate enough to be out with an experienced companion. You may be invited out to join a relative or friend who already shoots. You may seek or be given a chance to potter about over a piece of

ground on your own, or better still with a controllable dog.

In some instances a small group of friends and acquaintances may be involved, having obtained the shooting rights to an area of land where they may also rear and release a number of birds to help augment the wild stock. During the closed season they can share the duties of pest control, habitat improvement, ride clearing, hide building, crop protection and so on, so that there will be opportunities to be out and about with a gun, though with no guarantee of a shot, almost every week of the year. Out of season shooting can vary from organised outings to help reduce numbers of rabbits, grey squirrels or wood pigeons—all of which can offer excellent sport, with the added knowledge that a reduction in their numbers is helping protect crops and woodland—to a lone vigil trying to outwit a pair of carrion crows or magpies that will do untold damage to the resident game and songbird population if not controlled. With permission from the landowner and proper protection for the trap operator, there may even be a chance to use clay pigeons for some practice during the summer months.

In all these instances, two factors will be very different from the driven game situations. First and most obvious of course is the fact that much of the time will be spent walking around carrying a loaded gun, moving over all sorts of ground, and through different types of cover, with many obstacles to negotiate 'en route'. The second is that sometimes you may spend considerable periods of time crouched or seated in some sort of hide, perhaps decoying pigeons.

Make sure you know where your companions are before making any shot.

Putting your gun down

From time to time however, you will need to put down your gun in order to leave the hide, perhaps to re-arrange your decoys, to pick up shot birds or to attend a call of nature. As 'sod's law' dictates, whenever you have to move or do anything which entails putting down your gun, that will be the very moment a bird appears, even though you have seen nothing flying for at least half an hour. Nevertheless, you should never ever prop a loaded gun up in the corner of your hide while you attend to something else and you must be doubly careful if you have a dog in the hide with you. Even an unloaded gun, closed and propped up in a hide or anywhere else for that matter, will be at risk of being knocked over and having its stock broken or barrels dented and there is absolutely no point in blaming the dog for such an occurrence. If you have to leave the hide then either take the gun with you, unloading it before leaving or re-entering the hide, or unload it, leave it open and preferably lying flat on its cover or your game bag or something similar, while you attend to whatever you have to do. If you have laid down your gun,

Walking between sporting clays stands with guns safely open.

then, on getting back into the hide, remember to look through the barrels for any obstruction before reloading.

Walking up

Now, back to the first situation, that of walking up with a loaded gun, not really knowing when a shot might be offered or how much warning, if any, you might get. You may be out on your own or with a companion, a dog or both, so that not only must you look out for your own safety, but perhaps even more so, that of your companion or dog, so I make no apology for repeating these two rules. Firstly, as you walk around remember those two words: 'muzzle awareness'. Be conscious all the while, as you move around, of where your gun is pointing, not only while you are carrying it closed, but especially when opening or closing it to load and unload. Only last season I heard about a very experienced game shot who, standing at a peg, shooting driven pheasants with a top quality gun, accidentally killed his dog when his gun went off as he closed it. I can only imagine his horror and grief at what happened, but if he tried to blame the gun maker for the incident he would have been wrong to do so. I know that a gun should not go off as you close it, but I have seen it happen too many times. My own worst

experience of this was not with a shotgun but with a .375 magazine rifle which went off as I closed the bolt. This was on an approved range and happily the bullet did no more than plough a large furrow in the turf a few yards up the range. Any gun, no matter how good, can go off as it is closed. Metal parts, however well made or tempered, do wear and break down, usually with no prior warning; and no 'safety catch' is infallible. So remember please, close the gun pointing it safely towards the ground so that if by some mischance it does go off, it may well frighten the life out of you, but the shot will go harmlessly into the ground.

The second reminder is not to shoot where you cannot see the end result of your shot. With driven pheasants the golden rule was always to keep clear sky behind your targets. This is not so easy with grouse, but there, even when shooting against the heather, the butts are sited so that the beaters are protected until you get the signal that you must no longer shoot forward of the butts. Similarly when flighting duck or geese or roost shooting wood pigeons, most of the time you should have no trouble keeping sky behind the birds as you shoot. The exception may be with duck coming in very low against a high wind or perhaps catching you unawares in failing light, when before you shoot you must be absolutely certain that you know where any companions who are out with you are concealed and that once everyone is in their shooting positions, no-one moves out until some pre-arranged signal is given. Remember also that if shooting low over water, shot can ricochet in much the same way as it will from stony or frozen ground.

Variety of shots

When walking a piece of country, your background and horizon constantly change as you move up and down slopes, over open fields or through trees, so that you must keep monitoring the background against which you might shoot. You may flush a wide variety of potential targets, including game such as pheasants, partridges, hares, etc. which, providing

When walking a known piece of ground, use the natural cover to approach your quarry, being mindful of the background. Where would it be safe to shoot? Where would it not?

they are in season, that you have a current game licence if needed and that you have permission to shoot game over that ground, will offer a wide variety of shots: a pheasant rocketing obligingly up through tree tops so that it gives you a shot against the sky; a rabbit flushed from a clover ley, making a thirty yard dash for cover and giving a reasonable chance of a shot over open ground; the pheasant that never seems to get more than a couple of feet off the ground and is always on the other side of a hedgerow; a rabbit or woodcock giving

no more than a fleeting chance in thick cover. These last mentioned shots are the ones you must be most careful with, especially if you have a companion or dog working with you, so do keep monitoring the background cover all the while you are on the move. Think ahead, keep assessing and re-assessing the situation as you go along. Be on the look out constantly for potential hazards. Try to imagine what you would do if you suddenly put up a pheasant. Where would it be safe to shoot? Where would it not? If a rabbit flushes, see the clear spots where you might take it, the danger zones where you must not, e.g. against a hedgerow where you cannot see what is on the other side, close to the top of

With any form of clay target shooting protect your eyes as well as your ears.

a bank if you are down below, anywhere with livestock close by. In other words, anywhere where you cannot directly see where your shot will go. A little common sense and some practical observation helps also. For instance, if you are on your own working against the wind and you come across rabbits sitting out in the open, it is most unlikely that there is anyone else about ahead of you. (Remember that though you are out on your own, other people are about in the countryside, farm workers, ramblers who may have strayed from a footpath, horse-riders, people out mushrooming or blackberrying, courting couples. Many years ago I flushed one of the latter from a hayfield miles from anywhere, much to the embarrassment of all three of us!)

Birds such as jays, magpies and carrion crows getting up obviously alarmed by your approach are also good indicators that no one else is about. In the same way, on a known piece of territory, you will get used to knowing where opportunities of a shot might occur—in other words where you are likely to find or see your quarry. If nothing is seen sitting out in such places and if you are not scolded by the occasional jay or magpie, the chances are that someone or something else, possibly a fox, is out and

about also, so keep your wits about you; learn to develop that 'sixth sense'.

Gun mounting on a rough shoot

Many of the shots in these walk-up situations will make you feel rushed, especially if you are working through a patch of enclosing cover as opposed to being out in the open. Any target going away from you is likely to make you hurry. If you rush your gun mounting it will probably go wrong and result in a missed chance anyway, so what you need to do is practise. A cock pheasant bursting from cover, cackling as it goes, never fails to startle even if you know he is there beforehand. If you are not careful you will find that you have fired two harmless shots at a bird that is still no more than fifteen or twenty yards away.

What you need to do in order to make the most of these chances is practise your gun mounting to such an extent that you can bring up the gun accurately and unhurriedly without having to think about it. The secret is to bring the whole action down to an absolute minimum of movement by bringing the gun to the 'ready position' each time before mounting it. The ready position brings your muzzles under control by encouraging the pointing action of the front hand and discouraging the lifting action of the rear hand, this latter action being the main cause of bad mounting.

In most walk-up situations, both for the safety of anyone with you (including dogs), and because you are often going to be working through some sort of cover, the gun will normally be carried with the stock down and muzzles up, pointing safely skywards. This is one of the easiest positions from which to bring the gun up into the ready position as something flushes. All that is required is in fact the one thing you should not do during the actual mounting of the gun, that is to tuck the heel of the stock up under your armpit through lifting with the rear hand. Once the gun is tucked up well under your arm you can no longer lift with the rear hand. Then the action switches to the front hand which now has to push the gun out towards the target and away from your body in order to slide the stock up into your cheek. At the same time the shoulder moves in behind the stock in a shrugging motion to lock everything firmly into place just before the shot is fired. The actions of bringing the gun into the ready position and on into the shooting position will quickly blend into one smooth movement with a little disciplined practice, and the whole thing takes but a split second. You will get much more accurate results than you will if you try and throw the gun straight up to your shoulder from whatever position you are carrying it in when something gets up.

Practice

The practice needed can be done indoors or out and *it should go without saying that all practice must be done with an empty gun.* If you wish to practise pulling the trigger(s) as you complete the mount, then use good snap-caps to absorb the striker blows. Start practising from a standing position and, as with all mounting practice, the first thing to do is to pick out a point to look at, to concentrate on, to mount the gun onto. This is very important, as it is only by concentrating on a particular point as you mount the gun that you ensure that you keep your head still. If you do not pick a spot, all you will do is practise looking at

the gun each time you mount it—the last thing you need to do to make a successful shot! Start with a good stance, holding the gun in the sort of position you would have it when walking, concentrate on the spot you've picked to mount the gun onto, lift the stock up to tuck the heel well up under your armpit (the same action should bring the muzzles to a point just below the spot at which you are looking). Now push out with the front hand to bring the gun firmly up to your cheek and lock your shoulder in behind the butt.

Once you feel happy about mounting from the standing position, then you should try it while walking and this is best done outside always providing that you do not alarm the neighbours. To say you should practise mounting while walking is a little misleading as the first thing to do as something gets up is to stop walking. You will find that you can soon combine 'the stop' with 'coming into the ready position'. Out in the field you will often find that you are 'wrong-footed' when a bird rises. Even so, try to adopt a reasonable stance as you come into your 'ready position'. It is usually only a matter of moving one or other of your feet half a pace forward or backward.

There will be times though when you are well and truly caught out with perhaps one foot well above the other on a slope, one foot down a hole or caught in a briar, both feet stuck in mud. All you can do is make the best of each situation, so that once you are happy with your gun mounting, practise your body swing as well. Do this by picking out points to your left and to your right so that as you bring the gun into the 'ready position' you can already be turning your body slowly to face the target before you complete the mount. To take this exercise through to a logical conclusion—and so that you are not suddenly confronted with such a situation in the field without having thought it through—imagine a companion walking in line abreast with you, say thirty yards off to one side, with a bird either rising behind you and flying away or rising in front but flying back between you and your companion. The important thing now, if

Hazard of a different nature encountered while shooting sporting clays in San Antonio, Texas.

you decide to make a shot is of course to keep the gun muzzles pointing safely up as you turn past your companion before making any attempt to come into the 'ready position'. Once safely past him then the stock comes up under your arm as the muzzles come down onto the bird's line. Only then with the body still turning does the front hand push out to complete the mount.

There are many such exercises you can do, just by imagining the different situations in which you might find yourself. Practise mounting while seated as though in a hide. Go through each one in detail in your own mind, work out any safety problems then practise the combined gun mounting and body swing until you can do the whole thing safely and instinctively without feeling hurried.

Dealing with natural obstacles

As stated earlier, when walking around carrying a gun you will have to negotiate a variety of obstacles such as fences, hedges, slopes to scramble up or down, walls, ditches, fallen trees, plank bridges and many others. There is just one rule to follow, even if it means losing an opportunity to shoot: open and unload your gun while you cross over, under or through the obstacle. If you are alone, whenever possible lay down the open, empty gun under the fence or hedge you are crossing, not where you will jump on it as you go over, but in such a way that, when you pick it up from the other side, you can do so by getting hold of the stock. Never pull a gun through a fence or hedge by the muzzles. If you have to hold on to the gun while you cross over, then keep it open and take your time. Once over, check the barrels for obstructions before reloading. If you are with a companion, crossing these major obstacles is easier of course if you both cross at the same spot. First to cross gives his empty open gun to his companion, whose gun should also be open and empty. When number one is across, he takes both guns, still open and empty from number two; number two then crosses over to join his companion and reclaim his gun. In this way each one has both hands free to negotiate the obstacle.

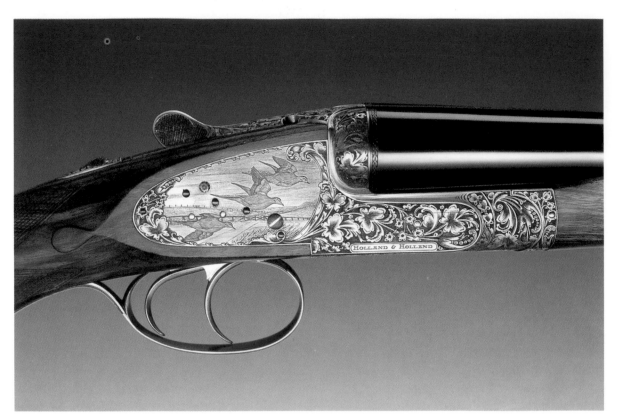

A 20-bore Holland and Holland 'Royal' deluxe with game scene engraving.

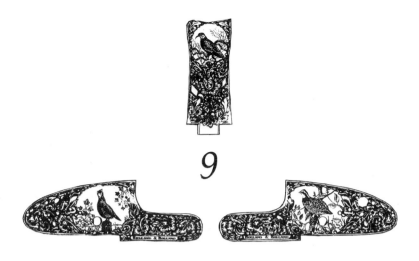

9

Ladies

DURING THE PAST ten years or so there has been a noticeable increase in the number of women shooting—some keen to shoot game, but many more of you are now enjoying clay target shooting of one sort or another.

In the USA the increase is even more marked due mainly to the sudden upsurge in popularity of sporting clays shooting there. They (our American cousins that is, not the ladies) may have been a little slow 'cottoning-on' to something we have been 'quietly' enjoying here for a very long while, but suddenly in the last few years they are making up for lost time at a tremendous pace and the ladies are joining in. Rather than stay at home while their men go off to shoot at the local gun club at week-ends they are joining their partners or getting out and having a go on their own. Long may the trend continue, as their attentive enthusiasm can brighten up the dullest of days for a flagging coach.

For any woman wanting to shoot, given suitable equipment, the determination to practise and some understanding guidance, there is no good reason why you should not go on to enjoy the sport and eventually compete on equal terms with most men. It is the starting out that may be difficult, there being a few extra problems for most of you to overcome.

Many women seem to have a natural in-built fear of guns to begin with—a fear of

the noise, or the recoil, maybe the memory of an incident years ago when some male 'allowed' you to try a totally unsuitable gun.

The average woman (if you'll excuse the expression) weighs less than the average man and possesses less upper body strength, an important factor when you may have to lift a gun weighing anything between six and eight pounds a hundred times or more.

The majority of women have opposite eye dominance so that few can shoot from their 'natural' side without doing something to counter the effect of the opposite eye.

If you are still with me after the last three paragraphs, and haven't rushed off thinking it would be easier to take up some more suitable pastime such as alligator wrestling, let's see what can be done to help.

To help counter these extra little problems you have one big advantage over most men—you listen to what is being said, whereas many men think they know it all already.

Taking the three points one by one, for 'natural in-built fear of guns' try substituting 'healthy respect for' and it sounds better already. Anything that makes a loud noise and kicks deserves some respect (how many of you ride horses?)

Just as when handling anything new and unfamiliar to begin with, a shotgun will feel awkward and unwieldly, even in the unlikely event of it being the right size and

Rather than stay at home while their men go off to shoot, the ladies are joining in.

shape for you. Before you ever attempt to shoot a gun, find out how it works. Get someone sympathetic to show you how to take one apart and re-assemble it; find out what each bit is called and what it does. Practise taking a gun apart and putting it back together until it becomes easy and familiar (preferably on an older gun which should go together more easily anyway, and where the odd little knock or scratch won't matter too much). Don't give up if a gun doesn't go together the first time you try. Persevere, without trying to force anything. If you feel you're having to force it, take it apart and start again. You should soon get the knack.

Once you decide to take a few shots, and those first few shots will often be very important in helping you decide whether to carry on or not, do use adequate hearing protection. There are many efficient plugs and muffs available, so that you will soon lose your fear of the noise. Keep your hearing protection in or on when standing close to anyone else shooting as the blast

from the muzzles of someone shooting alongside you can be worse than that from your own gun.

Overcoming the fear of recoil may not be quite so easy, especially if you have previously been hurt by an unsuitable gun or heavy cartridge. If you're very wary, start with the smallest gauge gun you can get hold of (.410 or 28 bore) and, unless you are about six feet tall, preferably one which has had the stock shortened and a recoil pad fitted. Wear something sensible, do not attempt to shoot in shirt sleeves. Try a reasonably thick sweater, or a shooting jacket with a shoulder patch, but don't put on so many layers that you cannot get the stock up into the right spot on your shoulder. If the gun you are going to use has no recoil pad, try to get hold of one of those that can be fastened inside your jacket or to your shirt and underneath your sweater. Those made from a material called 'sorbothane' need not be more than ¼ inch thick to be effective so will not get in the way when pinned inside a garment and are very efficient in dissipating recoil. You will also need a couple of snap-caps so that you can mount the gun and pull the trigger(s) a few times and so become familiar with the weight of the trigger pulls.

Here I need to re-cap and enlarge upon this last section. I stated elsewhere that over the years a 'standard' gun fit has evolved, but that standard fit has evolved for men. If you try out an 'off the shelf' gun, that has not been altered in any way, there is a good chance that at least two things will be wrong with the stock, both concerning its length. It is more than likely that the stock will be anything up to an inch too long overall and there will certainly be too much 'toe' on the stock. On guns without recoil pads the toe of the stock can be pointed, hard and sharp edged, a totally unsuitable shape for the anatomy of most women. If you have to begin with such a gun, do pin a recoil pad under whatever garment you have chosen to wear. Once you start shooting regularly, the sooner you get a stock of a reasonable length and shape the better. Please do not go on pounding the top of your breast with a sharp-toed gun. Not only will it be uncomfortable, but it cannot do you any good in the long run.

To help find the correct place for the gun on your shoulder, that pocket for the butt of the stock to fit into, first take up a good basic stance. A quick note here: women, due I believe to the shape of the pelvis, stand differently from men. Most tend to stand with the hips thrust slightly forward, so that the tendency is to lean back a little from the waist. This action tends to throw back the shoulders and make it difficult to get full contact with the butt of the stock. This tendency to lean back can become more exaggerated when given a heavy gun to hold; you will probably want to lean even further back to counter-balance its weight. To help overcome this, push your hips back, or put less politely stick your bottom out a little and lean forward slightly from the waist. This action should bring your whole body weight more forward over the balls of your feet and help you form a much better shoulder pocket in which to snuggle the gun butt. Now fold your arms and with the fingers of the opposite hand (which will now be lying just underneath this shoulder pocket) find

the inside edge of your shoulder joint, and your collar bone. These are two places you definitely do not want to shoot the gun from. Ideally the butt of the stock should lie inside the edge of your shoulder joint towards the chest, with the heel of the stock just below and clear of your collar-bone. At the lower end of the stock, depending on your shape, the toe will probably just touch the top of the breast, and it is in this area that the stock should be carefully contoured so as not to dig in each time a shot is fired. The butt of the stock in fact lies exactly on the line of your bra strap, so make sure that there are no hard rings or fastenings on the strap which will lie under the butt and get pushed into your flesh each time you fire a shot. Still on the same subject, when you go out to shoot, don't strap up too tight, no matter how good an impression you wish to make. Rather slacken things off a little and hang loose; it will make you a much better shape to mount your gun well.

You have one big advantage over most men, you listen to what is being said.

Efficient ear-plugs, worn here with shooting glasses and peaked hat, essential to protect ears and eyes.

Lean forward slightly from the waist to help keep your body weight forward over the balls of your feet, and your shoulder in behind the gun.

Remember when you bring up the gun to have the comb of the stock firmly against the fleshy pad of your cheek and not against your cheek-bone or lower jaw-bone.

Read through the sections on stance, holding the gun, 'ready' position and gun mounting again. Remember when you bring up the gun to have the comb of the stock firmly against the fleshy pad of your cheek and not against your cheek bone or lower jaw bone. Push your shoulder in behind the gun butt rather than pull the butt back into your shoulder and hold on firmly with your front hand so that the front arm can help absorb the recoil.

Before taking your first 'real' shots put a snap-cap in the gun and try following a few targets so that you get the feeling of moving along the flight line. You can then pull the trigger as you catch or overtake each target (depending upon which shot you elect to begin with) without harming the gun and without the distraction of noise or recoil. This preliminary exercise with a snap-cap is valuable for any beginner as it will give a good feeling for the movement involved, the timing of the shot and of course the weight of the trigger-pull so that you are not caught out by a premature discharge. Half a dozen targets followed in this way should be sufficient before you substitute a live cartridge for the snap-cap.

This lady means business. Total concentration, good starting position, perfect grip, nice natural head position.

When you take your first shots, load only one cartridge, and do so with the gun already mounted, making sure as far as possible that you have everything in a good position. If the mount does not feel good, come down and do it again. Do not fire too many shots to begin with. Ten or so may well be enough as your arms will tire quickly at this early stage, especially when starting with the gun already in your shoulder. If possible take these first shots at a reasonably straightforward on-coming or going away target so that hopefully as you become less conscious of the gun and more relaxed about what you are doing you can enjoy some early success. Build on this as soon as you feel able by starting the shot with the gun in the 'ready' position, bringing it up into the shooting position and, of course, pointing at the spot you wish to pick up the target, calling for the target just as you complete the mount. Go on to calling the target half way through the mount and finally to calling before you start

the mount (while the gun is still in the 'ready' position). Don't rush things and if it all goes wrong, take a break, go back a step, and work up again. A little and often is far better than one long session. You should soon be able to move up to a larger gauge gun (a 20 bore is generally as high as you need go if your choice is mainly to shoot game). If you really become serious about competing then you will probably finish up shooting a 12 bore gun, either an under-and-over or a semi-automatic of a weight to suit your build, with a cartridge that doesn't 'bite' too much.

Having decided on what stock length best suits you, if possible with some experienced help, when you have the stock shortened have a good quality recoil pad fitted, with the toe suitably reduced to sit well in your shoulder, and all the edges rounded down. The pad should be polished so that it slides easily up into position when you mount it, or else covered with thin leather for the same ease of mounting.

Take it easy to begin with, but once you decide that this is for you, get out and give the guys a run for their money.

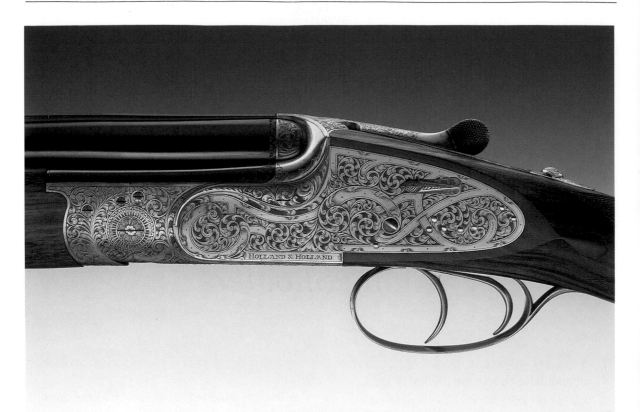

The new gun of the 1990's, a Holland and Holland sidelock over and under model. Incorporating many of the original Holland and Holland over and under patents, this 20 bore is designed for easy handling and loading in the game field and is the forerunner of a range which will include a gun specifically designed for sporting clay shooting.

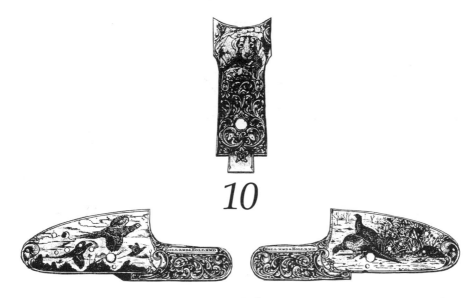

10

Young Shooters

To MY MIND, few experiences are more
rewarding than watching a keen
youngster respond well to good coaching.
The expression of delight on a young face
as that first, eagerly-sought target shatters,
has to be seen to be believed: the bright-
eyed enthusiasm to go on and repeat the
success; the visible increase in stature as
success builds confidence; the eager
questions as the lesson progresses. At the
end of such a session, both pupil and coach
will be mentally drained, but elated by the
whole experience.

On the other side of the coin, nothing is
more frustrating to both parties, than
trying to give a lesson to a youngster who
has clearly been pushed into the situation
against his will, usually by an overbearing
adult, a youngster who would quite plainly
be happy doing almost anything other than
take a shooting lesson. No-one will
respond well to such treatment; indeed he
or she may well be put off completely, and
lost from the sport for good, no matter how
expert the coaching. However anxious a
father may be for a son to take up his sport,
he should wait for the child to express an
interest. Some gentle guidance is fine, but
it is far better to wait another year or two,
than push too hard too soon.

Thankfully such instances are few and far
between as most parents are wise enough
to wait until a boy, or girl, expresses an
interest in shooting, rather than put them

into a situation they clearly do not wish to
be in.

A lack of interest must not be confused
with the perfectly natural reluctance, even
fear, some youngsters exhibit before
handling a gun for the first time and firing
those first few all-important shots. This is
where careful treatment is vital and much
depends on the experience of the coach.
Time must be taken to explain the basic
principles; to find a suitable gun and
cartridge combination along with efficient
hearing protection; to ensure that stock
placement at cheek and shoulder is good
and that the pupil has a reasonable
understanding of what to expect before
firing the first real shot.

During this introduction, some
youngsters will benefit from the moral
support lent by the presence of a parent
and it is often good for the adult to
experience the initial safety instruction and
basic gun handling techniques anyway.
After the introduction most youngsters are
then best left alone with the coach. This
way progress is usually much faster, as the
child will feel under less pressure and be
more relaxed. The continued presence of
another adult can often be counter-
productive, as the pupil will be trying
much too hard to please. There is also
nothing more irritating than 'helpful
interjections' from a third party standing
close behind, no matter how well meant

This bright-eyed young lady is ready for her lesson with a 28 bore gun.

possible, maintain the necessary level of concentration.

Second, and I think that this is perhaps the more important of the two, that he or she has a well enough developed sense of responsibility to realise just what they are about to be put in charge of, albeit under close supervision, and to realise just how much damage even a small-bore shotgun can do, especially at close range. An average starting age seems to be about eleven or twelve, but I have given lessons to eight- and nine-year-olds who have responded very well and shown an almost instinctive understanding of good, safe gun handling, right from the start. On the other hand, I have known fourteen- and fifteen-year-olds, who, no matter how many times they are told or shown, seem unable to grasp the basic idea of 'muzzle-awareness', and, because of this, would not be responsible enough to be out in the

This young man looks a little disappointed with himself, but he has already learned the safety rules well. His gun has been cleared before turning to walk off the stand, the breech is open and clear, with the muzzles pointing safely to the ground.

(usually just as coach and pupil are establishing that close contact and co-operation so necessary to get the best from one another).

Two of the most commonly asked questions by parents of prospective young shooters are: 'What is the best age at which to start?' and 'What is the ideal gun with which to begin?' Neither query can really be given a straight-forward answer as individuals vary enormously in both their physical and mental development. Once an interest in shooting has been expressed, the two most important factors are these: first that the child be developed well enough physically to handle the gun provided in a controlled manner, always taking into account the fact that frequent short rests should be given during early lessons anyway, often after every four or five shots, not only to rest young arms which can quickly become fatigued, but also to give the youngster a chance to absorb what is being said and, as far as

shooting field without the very strictest supervision.

As for the question, 'What is the ideal gun?' there is again no easy answer. Thoughts seem to turn automatically to the .410 and my heart sinks! Let me say right away that I am not condemning the .410 which, in expert hands, particularly when used with the 3" cartridge, can be a very effective weapon, but in my view, other than for the smallest and most nervous pupils, it is not the ideal gun with which to begin. I have watched too many youngsters, over the years, struggle to break targets with these small guns and the tiny pinch of shot they throw. As nothing succeeds like success, one of the most important things for a youngster to do is to break one or two targets fairly early on in a lesson, preferably within the first ten or so shots; he or she is then generally 'hooked'. Now it is not difficult to miss ten shots in a row, even on a relatively easy target, with a .410 and this does nothing to boost a youngster's confidence, no matter how much encouragement they may be given. Far better to begin with a 28 bore if possible. Most youngsters can handle this sweet-shooting little gun. Many can begin with, or at least move quickly on to, a 20 bore gun, providing always that the stock is of a reasonable length and shape and that a sensible cartridge is chosen. Resist the temptation to give a youngster an ultra-light gun; stay close to the average, well-tried weights of the bore size chosen and remember that the lighter the gun the more it recoils, whether it be .410 or 12 bore.

The choice of 'side-by-side' against 'under-and-over' will generally be a more personal one, depending to some extent on tradition and perhaps whether the coming opportunities for the youngster concerned are going to be mainly at game or purely clay target shooting.

Do not scorn the use of recoil-pads for the young—there is nothing 'macho' about getting bruised. In particular the type which can be pinned inside a jacket or shirt, as opposed to one fixed to the stock itself. Most youngsters will necessarily be using guns with shortened stocks, but will also be growing quickly during the first few years of shooting so that a stock will probably have to be lengthened once or twice, or the gun itself changed, so that fitting a recoil-pad to the stock each time may not be practical. A thin pad, pinned snugly inside a garment, should not impede good gun mounting—a plain rubber pad on the gun-stock itself, unless well polished or covered in leather, surely will.

A keen youngster is a pleasure to teach and everything possible should be done to encourage them. Always remember that today's young shooter is tomorrow's adult and as such holds the future of our sport in his or her hands.

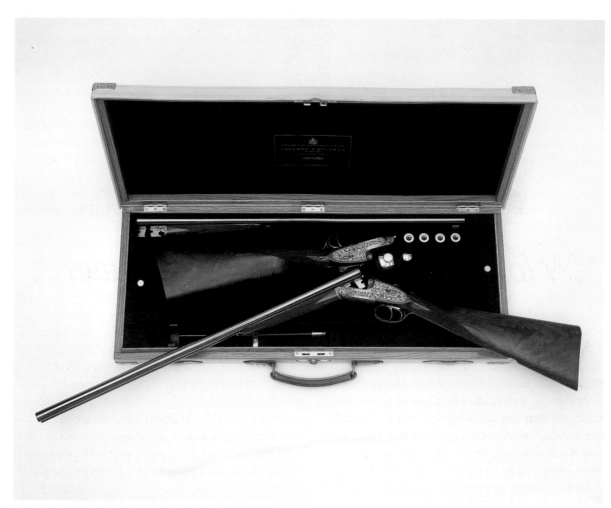

A pair of new Holland & Holland 12 bore 'Royal' de luxe guns, displayed in their double oak and leather case.

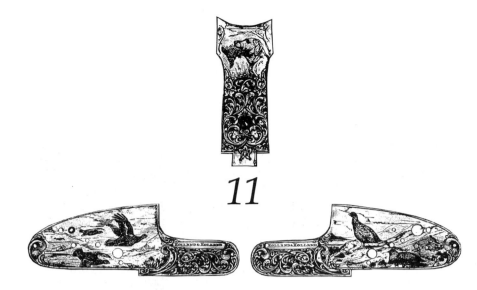

11

Working two guns with a loader

ALTHOUGH there are fewer genuine opportunities to use a pair of guns on driven gamebirds these days, there are still occasions—especially in a good grouse year—when not only to harvest a valuable crop successfully, but also for the health of the stock the following year, their use is called for and you may suddenly find yourself called upon to bring along a second gun. Many sportsmen visiting from overseas are also encouraged to travel with two guns, an excellent idea in itself, for to travel thousands of miles with a single gun only to have it break down unexpectedly can spoil an expensive trip. Whatever the reason for being asked to use two guns, if it is something new to you the following section will I hope help both shooter and loader do things correctly.

Safe, successful shooting with a pair of guns depends very much upon both shooter and loader working well together as a team. Watched at its best it can be poetry in motion, with the shooter able to look forward and concentrate on his targets, knowing that when he reaches across for his second gun it will be placed accurately and firmly (though not heavily) into his leading hand as the first gun is taken smoothly away; he should also know that when he turns to take shots on either side, or even directly behind, that his loader will not impede him and should be confident in the knowledge that, while

watching what is going on in front, his loader is not covering the backs of his legs or anyone else in the line with the second gun.

At its worst it becomes a comic dance, occasionally a dangerous one, where the shooter is constantly on the move, darting back and forth or to right and left, usually for no good reason, while the frustrated loader vainly attempts to follow. The results are inevitable—gun barrels clash together during the changes, sometimes resulting in the need for expensive repair work, cartridges are dropped, guns not reloaded in time and words may be exchanged as tension mounts between the two would-be 'partners'.

As said at the start, shooter and loader should work together as a team, each with his own responsibilities, confidently and unhurriedly going about their separate tasks, each confident in the other, so that together they work like a well-oiled machine.

The shooter's role
As the shooter you must stay on one spot, which is not a problem when shooting from inside the confines of a grouse-butt for instance. But, when on a numbered peg waiting for pheasants or partridges, having decided just where to stand and after clearing away any débris from underfoot, unless given specific instructions to move

1 *Loader facing the rear and in possession of both guns. Shooter looking suitably disinterested. The gun under his left arm is open and unloaded. Gun under his right arm has been loaded and is being closed safely towards the ground with the right hand pushing up from underneath as he leans forward over it. The stock is locked between his body and right arm.*

2 *The loader has turned safely through the line with the muzzles of the loaded gun safely upright. This is the only time the loader passes a gun while holding it near the fore-end, and the only time the shooter takes it by the grip with his rear hand. Second gun still open and unloaded.*

3 *Both shooter and loader ready for action. Guns loaded and pointing skyward. Loader is close in behind shooter's right shoulder, facing slightly right in order to turn easily through the line to his right as he re-loads.*

4 *By bending his knees and leaning back the loader can stay in close attendance and watch what is going on if he is 'shot spotting', ready to make the change.*

as the drive progresses, stay put. For your loader to work safely and efficiently he needs to be able to stand close in behind whichever shoulder you shoot from, not only so that guns can be passed back and forth easily, but perhaps even more importantly so that he can side-step to right or left in order to keep out of harm's way as you turn to take shots at birds passing through the line. If you suddenly move a yard or two from your chosen spot without warning, you may find yourself face to face with him as you turn for those shots behind the line—your fault, not his. On shooting behind the line, do not attempt to change guns when in this turned-around position; it only makes for a tangle of arms and gun-barrels. It is far easier and quicker in the long run to turn back again to face the front in order to make an orthodox change over. Indeed, wherever you turn to take a shot you should return to this frontal position whenever possible while changing guns, so helping develop and practise the co-ordinated routine so necessary between yourself and your loader for a good working relationship.

Safety in exchanging guns
The actual exchange of weapons is very straightforward providing both parties obey a few basic rules. As the one shooting it is your responsibility, and yours alone, to work the safety-catches on the guns; your loader should not have to touch them and should never be requested to do so. Whether the guns you are using have automatic or non-automatic (manual) safety-catches, your loader should hand them to you with the catches in the 'safe' position and this is the mode in which you must hand them back to him. The action of sliding back the catch to 'safe' must be done each time before you change guns, regardless of whether one or both shots have been fired. Remember that in order to keep a fully-loaded gun in your hands whenever possible, you will often be handing back to your loader a gun

containing an unfired cartridge.

To effect the change over, bring the stock down from your shoulder, pulling back the safety-catch as you do so and let go of the gun with your leading hand. As you release the barrels from the leading hand pivot the gun upright in your rear hand so that the muzzles point safely vertically up into the air. As the gun pivots upright draw your rear hand close into your chest. This will bring the fore-end of the gun near your ear and you will have 'opened the door' through which your loader can pass the second gun. The front hand, as it releases the barrels, is reached across your chest with palm outstretched ready to receive the second gun. If, at the same time, you turn your whole body slightly around in the direction of your loader, you will help both him and yourself make an easier, more efficient exchange. While all this is going on, your loader, who should be close in behind and just off to the side of the shoulder you are shooting from, is hopefully waiting attentively to complete the exchange. As your used gun is brought upright and close into your body, he will take it firmly from you, taking hold of it by the barrels at a point near the front of the fore-end as with his other hand he places the loaded gun into the outstretched palm of your leading hand. Ideally the gun should not be slapped down hard into your hand as this quickly becomes tiring on your front arm; rather it should be given a little forward and upward movement as you receive it, this being far less tiring. As, but not before, you feel your loader take possession of the first gun you can release it with your rear hand which should now be brought onto the grip of the second gun, which you have just received in your front hand, and you are straightway ready for action again.

If you are with a loader you do not know then go through the gun changing routine once or twice while waiting for the first drive to get under way, preferably with empty guns so that you get used to each others' ways. If it is your first time using a

The loader in this sequence of photographs is left-handed which is why he favoured wearing the cartridge-bag over his right shoulder. Apart from that he managed very well.

5 *After shooting, bring back the safety-catch as the gun comes down from the shoulder. Release the gun with front hand, bring the muzzles upright and*

6 *the gun back close to your body. Loader moving in to take fired gun in his left hand and pass second gun.*

7 *Loader has firm grip on fired gun with his left hand before shooter releases it. Loaded gun firmly placed in shooter's leading hand before being released by loader.*

8 *Shooter's right hand coming onto grip of stock. Loader now has both hands on the fired gun keeping it upright in order to turn through the line.*

pair of guns then say so—just keep your fingers crossed it isn't his first time as well! With practice there will be no need to look back at your loader while changing guns. You should be able to continue to watch what is going on around as the guns are passed back and forth.

What to expect of a loader

On a more general note your loader is there to help you, to keep you safely supplied with a loaded gun whenever possible during the drives and he should see to it, always providing you have arranged a sufficient supply of cartridges to begin with, that he keeps cartridge magazines and bags topped up as the day goes on. At the end of the day he will carefully clean and put away your guns in the gunroom ready for the next day, or back in your vehicle for the journey home. In addition, an experienced loader, especially on his home ground, can be helpful in that he will know the drives and the way the birds tend to come. This can be very helpful in a line of grouse butts where he can act as a spotter during the waits between the action. He may also be able to see shot accurately and perhaps help mark the birds down, but this is not something you should come to expect. During most of the action your loader will himself be busy changing and reloading guns, often with his back to the shooting in order to keep you supplied at all times, so take any shot spotting and so on as a bonus. Remember also that an almost automatic response to the question, 'Where did I miss that one?' rightly or wrongly is, 'You were behind it sir!' simply because he may feel embarrassed admitting he does not know. Remember he is there as your loader not as your coach. It is a different situation if you employ your own regular loader who you know can accurately see shot, especially if he has been along with you to a shooting ground a few times and has also got to know the mistakes you are likely to make.

Finally if you have an admiring onlooker with you or a dog or dogs then stand or sit them where they will not only be safely out of your way but out of your loader's way as well.

The loader's role

Reversing the roles, if you are acting as loader, then as previously stated your main duty is to keep your shooter safely supplied with a fully-loaded gun whenever possible. In order to do this, once the shooting begins you need to stand close in behind and just off to one side of whichever shoulder your 'man' shoots from, facing slightly to your right or left depending on which way you have decided to turn through the line to re-load. You should be able and prepared to turn either way as circumstances alter, but if loading for someone shooting from the right shoulder the more orthodox turn for the loader to make is to the right, even though, just as when shooting, this is a slightly more awkward movement to make, which is why standing facing slightly right will help. If you are loading for a right-hander and have to turn to your left to re-load, then care must be taken not to eject fired cases at and around him each time you open a fired gun. Apart from enabling you to turn through the line to re-load the guns safely behind, your stance should also allow you to side-step neatly to left or right when needs be and to keep down out of harm's way if shots are taken directly behind over your head while you are busy re-loading. When side-stepping to left or right, or when turning through the shooting line to re-load or return to your waiting position keep the muzzles of the gun you are holding pointing absolutely straight up in the air so that at no time during the entire operation do you cover the person you are loading for, anyone else in the shooting line, anyone in the beating line, any onlooker, dog or picker-up. The same applies as you open and close the guns as you re-load, these actions should be carried out with the muzzles pointing towards the ground behind the shooting line three or four feet away from your own toes; and just as though you yourself were doing the shooting, remember those same two words, 'muzzle awareness'. Remember also to glance quickly over your shoulder before turning back with the re-loaded gun in order to check that your shooter is not about to shoot behind the line.

9 *Shooter in full possession of loaded gun. Loader has turned safely through the line with gun still pointing up in the air.*

10 *Loader has opened gun safely behind the line and is crouched slightly so that shots can be taken over his head if necessary while he re-loads.*

11 *Gun being closed safely towards the ground behind the line, loader glancing back to make certain he does not get in the way as he turns back.*

12 *Loader has brought muzzles of re-loaded gun safely upright before turning back through the line to assume his waiting position.*

Preparing for a drive

As you arrive at the peg for the start of each drive you will in all probability be laden with two guns in their slip-covers, one or two bags filled with cartridges and possibly another bag containing water-proofs and any other kit you may require during the day. If the shooter you are accompanying arrives with you, or is already waiting at his peg eager to have a gun in his hands then this can make life a little easier. Put everything down carefully a yard or two behind or to one side, but never in front of the peg, and preferably not in any mud. Take one gun from its cover, check that both barrels are free from obstruction, load it with a couple of cartridges from the pocket in which you always carry a few extras and, with muzzles safely skyward, give him the gun. Now get yourself organized as quickly and quietly as possible. Put on the cartridge bag you wish to use, open it and tuck back the lid out of the way. The bag should be nicely filled, but not overflowing when all you will do is spill unfired cartridges under your feet as you move around. (By the way if you do drop cartridges while loading leave them until the drive is over, kick them aside if they are in the way but do not try to bend down and grovel about for them with a gun in one hand.) Take the other gun from its cover, open it and check the barrels as you did with the first one and take up your position close in behind your shooter. Load the second gun but do not close it; instead put it under your arm, the open (but loaded) barrels over your fore-arm and pointing safely towards the ground in just the way you would carry your own open gun over your fore-arm. From this position if there is a long wait before the drive gets going you have a hand free to take the loaded closed gun, keeping the muzzles always upright, from the shooter for a minute or two if he needs to rest his arms or perhaps sit on his shooting-seat for a while until things get going.

Dealing with both guns

If you arrive first at the peg, perhaps because your shooter has stopped for a gossip somewhere else along the line, or if he is with you at the peg, but it is clear that he wants nothing to do with a gun until the drive gets going, then you have a further complication to contend with, that of holding, loading and closing at least one of the guns while in the possession of both. It is not that difficult if you use your common sense and take a little care not to knock the two sets of barrels together, but in order to simplify this rather long explanation I am going to assume a right-handed loader loading for a right-shouldered shooter. This time the first thing to do after carefully setting down all the equipment is to put on and organize your cartridge bag. Ideally it should hang from your left shoulder with the strap lying diagonally across your back and chest down towards your right hip. The bag itself is best adjusted to lie in front of the hip resting against the top of your thigh so that you can reach in and out easily and can use the mouth of the bag to take the butt of the stock during a long wait. Next, open both covers, take out one gun, open it and check for obstructions, leave it open and unloaded and tuck it under your left arm with the barrels lying over your left fore-arm but leaving your left hand free. Slide the second gun from its cover with your right hand, grasping its barrels from above somewhere near the end of the fore-end with your left hand as you do so. In this position the two sets of gun barrels will become crossed over, the barrels of the gun over your left forearm above, but kept well clear of the barrels of the second gun which are still held firmly from above in your left hand. Continue to hold the second gun firmly in your left hand by the barrels while you open it with your right hand. Check the barrels for obstruction and, if clear, load it with your right hand but do not yet close it; instead tuck the stock under your right arm, bringing your right fore-arm around underneath the gun just in front of the trigger-guard, let go of the second gun with your left hand and uncross the two sets of barrels carefully. You now have full possession of both guns, one under each arm with the trigger-guards resting behind your fore-arms. Both guns are open but the one under your right arm is loaded. When

13 *Loader's stance close in behind shooter enables him to—side-step right as shooter turns left. . .*

14 *side-step left as shooter turns right. . .*

15 *crouch down behind as shooter takes shot directly over his head as he re-loads.*

16 *Trying to change guns with the loader while in a turned around position after shooting behind the line only makes for a tangle of arms and gun barrels. Always try to return to your frontal position before making the change over.*

the time comes to give the shooter his first gun, assuming you are facing the front, pivot to your right in order to close the loaded gun (the one under your right arm) safely behind the line. To do this keep the gun stock held firmly between the top of your right arm and your side. Support the gun from below as much as possible with your fore-arm as you move your right hand forward to grasp the gun barrels from underneath, somewhere near or just beyond the end of the fore-end in order to be able to exert a reasonable amount of leverage on the gun. Lean forward a little over the gun you are closing, the stock still locked under your right arm, push up from underneath with your right hand and you should be able to close the gun while keeping it pointing safely towards the ground. Before turning around make sure you have a good grip on the closed gun with your right hand, release the stock from under your right arm and turn the gun upwards to point the muzzles safely in the air before turning through the line to hand over the first gun. This is the only time (when you are in possession of both guns) that you will hand over a gun holding it near the fore-end in your right hand so that the shooter can take it by the grip, in his right hand. All the other changes should be made as described earlier. You can now load the second gun in the normal way and take up your waiting position in readiness to make the first change over. During long pauses you can take the weight of the gun by supporting the butt end of the stock on the top of your thigh, on your hip, or if you adjust your cartridge bag correctly, in the mouth of the bag itself, being careful not to mark the gun-stock on the brass buckle of the bag. For a similar reason it is not normally good practice to hold two, or multiples of two cartridges in between the fingers of one or both hands as you change guns and re-load as you will inevitably mark the stocks or fore-ends or both with crescent-shaped indentations from the metal heads of the cartridges. If you keep your bag topped up and spend a few moments during any lulls in the action to arrange the top layer of cartridges 'brass up' in the bag, you will

load just as quickly and without the risk of bruising what may well be the owner's exhibition grade gun-stocks. During the actual change over, firstly make sure that you take a firm grip on the used gun you are about to take away, especially if the weather is wet and cold. Secondly as you place the loaded gun into your shooter's leading hand, try to do it in such a way that he does not then have to change his grip. After watching him take a few shots you will soon see where he likes to hold the gun.

Handguards

If the pair of guns being used is supplied with handguards be particularly careful as you pass the guns back and forth. A handguard used on a single gun is fine; it locates the hand, prevents burnt fingers and can easily be re-positioned by the shooter if it moves forward on the gun as shots are fired. Handguards on a pair of guns though can be extremely dangerous. It is almost impossible without an actual fastening on the gun, to prevent a handguard from slipping towards the muzzles as shots are fired, and, as gun barrels taper down to the muzzles, a handguard can suddenly become loose creating a very dangerous situation, either as you take the fired gun away by the barrels (often still containing one unfired cartridge), or as you place the second gun into the shooter's leading hand. In both instances the guns are pointing upright for safety, but if in either situation the gun is grasped by the handguard there will be a moment when each gun is being held only at this one point and a previously safe manoeuvre can turn into a disaster as the gun slides down through the loose handguard with the very real danger of it going off as the butt hits the ground. I really do not think that handguards should be used when shooting two guns; far better and safer for the user to wear a good thin leather glove on the front hand and just occasionally in a really hot corner, you as the loader might need to do the same. As with any other activity, the more familiar you become with it, the more you can practise, the more efficient you will become.

Mistakes commonly made when first working with a pair of guns:

17 Shooter opening gun after shooting instead of bringing it into upright position ready to make the change over.

18 Shooter letting go of the gun with the wrong hand.

19 Shooter allowing barrels or fired gun to hang out to his right side, effectively 'closing the door' to the loader.

Useful extras for a loader

A few useful items carried on your person or tucked away in the bag in which you keep your waterproofs and such like can help earn a few extra 'brownie points'. Apart from the proverbial piece of string and a good sharp pocket knife, here is a list of things I normally take along when loading: whether or not you smoke, matches or a lighter; a bubble-pack of aspirin or something similar; a good pair of tweezers, useful for removing thorns from human hands or doggy-paws; a small selection of band-aids; a travel pack of tissues, and although fewer and fewer people use paper-cased cartridges these days, I still carry a universal extractor with me.

Finally, if one of the guns being used develops a fault, do not keep using it, put it safely away and prepare to become what is normally termed these days 'a stuffer'. It is in fact just as quick—for an inexperienced shooter even quicker—to work with a single gun and have none of the worry of doing something wrong during the changes.

Reversing the roles again, all that is then necessary is that as the shooter, you open the gun decisively and fully as you bring it from your shoulder, trying not to hit your loader in the eye with the ejected cases, easily achieved by turning the gun over slightly to the outside as you open it. Hold the gun open, keep it turned slightly over and *keep it still* by locking the stock against your hip with your forearm. Pivoting your body a little towards the loader will help him reach the chambers and, although you can keep watching the front, just as when using two guns, try not to close his fingers in the breech.

Some common mistakes

The most likely mistakes for the (inexperienced) shooter to make when first using two guns are:
a) Forgetting to pull back the safety-catch before making a change over, something the loader should look out for and advise about.
b) Opening the gun after shooting—an almost automatic reaction if you have been used to shooting a single gun for any length of time. In this situation you have two choices: *Either* leave the gun open, let go with your front hand and reach it across your chest, when your loader will then be able to pass the second gun in the usual way, dealing with the opened gun as best he can when he takes it from you. At least it will be open with muzzles down as he turns through the line. *Or*—and this may be your only option in a grouse-butt—close the gun carefully and bring it upright again in your rear hand to make the change.
c) Letting go of the gun with the rear hand instead of the front hand as you bring it to the upright position. Not much you can do here other than change hands on the gun again or let the loader take the gun from your front hand before putting the second gun into it. Do not make a snatch for the second gun with your rear hand.
d) Failing to bring the barrels upright, allowing them to hang out to the side. This is effectively 'closing the door' for your loader, an almost certain way to dent one or both sets of barrels.

In any of the above situations try not to panic, take your time, think the process through and thank heaven for a considerate loader.

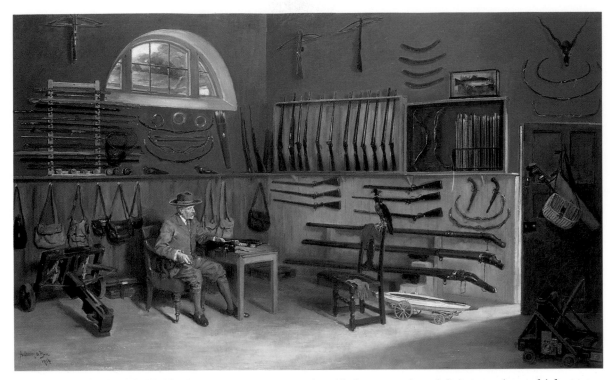

Not all gunrooms can boast the bows, boomerangs, Indian chakrams and model siege engines which are displayed in Sir Ralph Payne-Gallwey's impressive armoury of sporting firearms. This oil painting of Thirkleby Hall in Yorkshire was painted by Anthony de Bree two years before Sir Ralph, widely regarded as one of the leading authorities on shooting of the late Victorian and Edwardian age, died in 1916. The painting, now held in the Holland & Holland Collection, is on view in the Company's Gunroom in Bruton St, London.

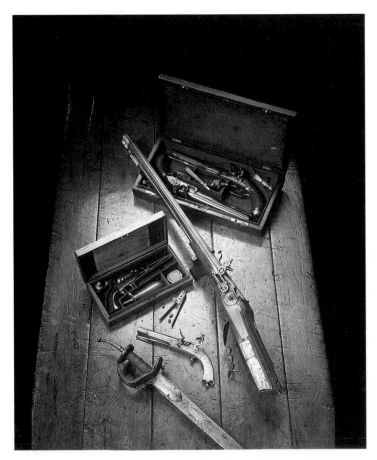

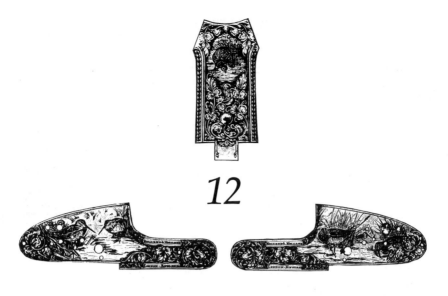

12

Gun Care

WITH the advancement of technology the care and maintenance of the shotgun is not the time-consuming chore of yesteryear. Cleaner burning powders, non-corrosive primers, modern spray oils with their high capillary action, silicone impregnated cloths, all have helped reduce the effects of corrosion on sporting guns and rifles when in use in the field and while in store between seasons.

There is little point in going through a detailed description of cleaning a gun after use as this is normally a very straightforward process with each user developing his own set routine, with a little more attention to detail being necessary if the gun has become wet. There are plenty of good cleaning kits available, most dealers supplying one with the gun.

Use of oil

The objective during this cleaning being to leave the inside surface of each barrel clear of any fouling, polished and very lightly oiled and the outside surfaces wiped clean of any dirt or moisture (including perspiration which from some individuals quickly causes rust marks). Again the outside surfaces should be left lightly oiled. For this reason try to let the oily duster used to wipe off the barrels at the end of the process be the last thing to touch them as you put them away. For the stock and fore-end carefully wipe them dry after use

in any wet situation; a roll of kitchen tissue is ideal for this as it quickly blots up any moisture. Any mud which has got into the chequering can be removed gently using an old clean tooth brush and working along the lines. If the stock has become very wet a very small amount of linseed oil, *never ordinary gun oil*, should be worked in with the fingers and palm of your hand, keeping well away from the chequering and wiping off any excess not readily absorbed. On extremely wet days the head of the stock can swell—should this occur allow it to dry naturally at room temperature. Do not apply artificial heat which might cause the wood to crack or twist if dried too quickly. For similar reasons do not store your guns too close to any source of central heating which might dry out the oil from the wood causing it to twist, crack and become brittle. Wipe over the metal parts of the stock and fore-end with your oily duster leaving the thinnest possible film of oil. Keep this oil away from the woodwork and do not go squirting quantities of oil into every nook and cranny you can find. Over-oiling is worse than under-oiling; excess oil on the action and in the locks will eventually gum up the works and finish up soaking back into the end grain of the wood at the head of the stock, weakening and discolouring it. Gun oil rots wood and many older guns have had their stocks spoiled through years of being over-oiled and then stood, muzzles up, in a gun cabinet so that the oil runs back through the action into the head of the stock, sometimes soaking back several inches towards the grip. This oil in the wood renders useless the adhesive properties of any glues which could otherwise be used to effectively repair any small splits or cracks which might appear in the wood around the locks and action of the gun during its lifetime. For the above reasons the stripping, cleaning and servicing of guns by gunmakers ends with a light grease, not oil, being applied to the lock-work.

Barrels

A number of other observations on gun care are worth noting. The most vulnerable part of a gun are its barrels. They are prone to more damage than any other part of the sporting gun. They are also the foundation of, and primary consideration for, any evaluation of a gun, be it a top class sidelock or cheaper variety of boxlock. Care of the barrels is therefore crucial. Thousands of cartridges fired through the gun will make no difference to the internal diameters of the barrels, but the repair of dents, bulges and the re-fixing of ribs will of course enlarge the bores, each repair bringing the gun closer to its proof limits.

A problem sometimes overlooked is one which may occur after shooting on cold winter days. At the end of the shooting, barrels are cleaned and put away cold into their cases which are themselves then put into a car which has been standing out most of the day in the cold. If the day is damp as well as cold, not unusual during a British winter, the heat in the car on the drive home can cause moisture to condense on the barrels inside the case as the air in the car warms up. Left in this condition the barrels will be red with rust within a week, so, on arriving home, check the gun and wipe the barrels over again before putting it away in your gun-safe.

Opening and closing

Check for unusual sounds when opening and closing the gun. A clicking sound on a sidelock gun heard during this operation could indicate that part of the connecting piece between the mainspring and the tumbler, a part called the swivel, could be damaged. Left unattended this can cause the tumbler to break. It is much cheaper to fit a new swivel than a new tumbler.

Guns which may quite suddenly become difficult to close fully, despite the fact that no obvious cause such as dirt or débris of some sort can be found in the action or behind the extractors, if examined closely may be found to have a loose extractor stop-pin. This small screw is located in the lumps of the barrels and may become loose to such a degree that it comes into contact with the bottom of the action, so preventing the gun from closing fully. Such a gun, if forced closed, may be damaged by the head of the loosened screw indenting the bottom of the action. As a temporary solution a drop of 'loctite' may be applied to the screw before tightening it down, but as soon as possible have your gunmaker fit a new stop-pin.

Chambers

There are numerous complaints these days of ejectors being weak and of cartridges only being extracted half way from the chambers of older guns, an irritating occurrence during a busy drive and inevitably the gunmaker who last serviced the gun is blamed. However, this problem can be caused by the crimped part of the plastic cartridge case (used so widely these days), which has been blown open by the discharge, bearing down hard against the chamber cones. Many of these guns were, of course, chambered 40, 50 and 60 years ago for the paper-cased 2½" cartridge and the cone of the chamber produced then is much shorter than that used by gun manufacturers today. One remedy, therefore, is to increase the length of the chamber cone (not the length of the chamber itself which would render the gun out of proof), in order to ease the situation.

To conclude, I recommend that at the end of the season you let your gunmaker examine and report on your gun to see if anything is wrong or about to go wrong.

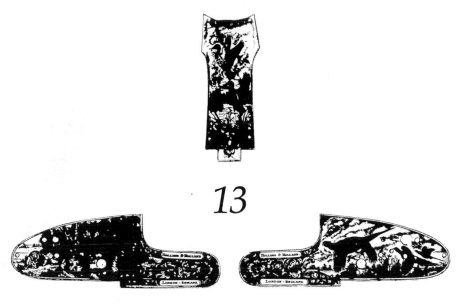

13

Conclusion

WHAT I HAVE endeavoured to do in this book is to give you, stage by stage, a comprehensive description of a well-proven method of shooting a shotgun at moving targets. It is not the only method in use, though when you break down most of the others they are remarkably similar in many ways, sometimes the only difference being that of individual interpretation. Along with the method, the safe-handling chapter is very important so if you were tempted to skip through it, go back and read it again thoroughly. With a growing number of voices raised against the ownership and use of shotguns, whether for game or clay pigeon shooting, it is vitally important that you learn to handle them safely and wisely, help set an example for others, and don't bring disrepute to your chosen sport. Learn to respect your quarry and the countryside you shoot over. Above all look out for the safety of others when out with your gun, and if in doubt about any shot, don't take it. No matter how well you shoot, one careless act can spoil the day (and much more) for all concerned and will take you a long while to live down.

A reasonable gun fit is important in order to get the best from whatever method or combination of methods you use. Remember though that for the majority of adult males, the 'off the shelf' gun will normally come close to a 'fit' and that you should develop your technique through practice before worrying too much about detailed gun fitting. For the minority who will need stock shapes markedly different from the 'norm', this need should become apparent quite quickly if you are shooting regularly, either because you are not hitting relatively straightforward targets even though you feel you are mounting the gun well, or if you are perhaps being knocked about by the gun. Seek some advice from a reputable shooting ground or gun club. It may well be that your technique is still at fault, not the gun, so that a single lesson may be all that is needed to put you on the right track. If your technique is sound then it should not be too difficult to assess your correct gun fit. If your technique is unsound then of course it will not be possible to make a definitive fitting until you do something about it. A good well-fitting gun is a joy to use, but do not become obsessed with stock fitting. A fitted stock may be important but it is no 'cure-all'. It is certainly no substitute for the disciplined, dedicated practice needed if you want to make it to the top.

Few people shoot well enough or often enough to be able to appreciate small differences (say an eighth of an inch either way) in stock length or bend at heel—though they may well notice a lack of cast. So there is absolutely no point in playing around with sixteenths or thirty-seconds of an inch in the length or bend of your stock.

Look at their eyes and you see a pretty mean machine. Confident, aggressively so.

An exception to this may be among some of the top trap shooters, where, because of the 'gun up' start made for each shot, they become very conscious of stock size and shape, and of their eye-line over the top-rib, not to mention recoil, so that they may well benefit from the tiny individual 'tweaks' many make to their guns. Tiny alterations which the average person shooting could not possibly feel, let alone appreciate, can, in an off-shoot of the sport which is extremely precise and demanding, give a much needed confidence boost to help score that perfect round or perhaps help salve a bruised ego after an off day.

Going back to the method, the basic principles are very simple: use your own natural hand and eye co-ordination in much the same way as you do when playing a ball game, throwing a stone, dropping a fly over a fish, or just screwing up a piece of paper and tossing it neatly into a waste basket ten feet away without thinking how you do it. The trouble starts when you *quite deliberately* screw up that second piece of paper and *try* to toss it in

the basket. Suddenly it becomes much more difficult to do simply because you have begun to think about it. This is where practice is important, so that you can go on to repeat the series of actions involved in making a successful shot time and again without having to think hard about them.

If you ask a good shot how he does it, the chances are he won't be able to tell you. He may well tell you in all good faith what he thinks he does, but if watched carefully and analysed, it may in fact not be what he does at all. Whatever you do, do not ask this question of anyone half way through a good drive or during a competition, as they certainly won't thank you for it. Unless they are very experienced, the fact that you have made them think about what they are doing will almost inevitably cause a miss.

The seasoned game shot will have gained, and subconsciously stored, a tremendous amount of information to draw upon as he shoots, experiences gained over many years in the game field under widely varying conditions of wind and weather. There are times when he may not be called upon to repeat the same shot twice throughout a whole day, let alone in a single drive, yet subconsciously he knows how to deal with a particular target when it presents itself. The information gained in the past to make such a shot well, is filed away in his own very personal computer. Here there is a similarity with tossing that first piece of paper in the basket. Presented suddenly with a particular shot he may not have made for years, subconscious memory is instantly recalled, used successfully, reinforced and stored away again. The trouble would start if that same target was repeated ten times in succession. He would then probably begin to think about it, wonder how he did it and lose it.

Between seasons

Most people shooting game these days (perhaps I should qualify that and say 'driven game') shoot comparatively little. Six to ten days out during a whole season being as much as most will manage, so that it can become difficult to gain sufficient experience to fall back on when needed. For many, the season ends just as they are getting into their rhythm, with a wait of nine months or so until the next one comes around. Then what happens? They put away their game guns with never a thought about some out-of-season practice in order to stay familiar with the handling of the gun during such a long let-up. There are a few wise ones and some who will take a quick crash course just before each season starts, to get back into the swing of things, but most seem content almost to start over again as each new season begins.

Whatever anyone tells you, well-presented clay targets, shot regularly and accompanied now and again by some good coaching, can very definitely help your game shooting. No, it's not quite like the real thing. You cannot get the same excitement and thrill, that run of adrenalin you experience out in the field, but the very fact that you are handling the gun regularly, watching, assessing and shooting at a variety of well-presented moving targets, cannot fail to help. Your gun mounting will improve, as will your reactions and timing, and, as an added bonus, if anything odd is happening to your eye-sight which might warrant a change in technique or gun fit, you will be

fore-warned and able to do something about it before the next season begins.

Competition game clays

In contrast the experienced competitor will often shoot throughout the year, practising regularly, working to reach peak form in time for major competitions, sometimes also shooting game in season or wood-pigeons whenever possible. His problems are somewhat different from the game shooter in that each time he steps onto a stand he knows he is about to make a series of shots, usually at known targets, very often having to repeat the same two shots a number of times and hold onto the concentration needed to do so.

How easy it is to walk onto a stand, shoot the first two or three pairs well and make a complete mess of the last two or three, even though moments earlier you were reducing similar targets to dust. So what goes wrong? Usually the problem lies between the ears. Maybe the first two pairs felt so easy that you relaxed too much, became a little blasé about the whole thing, did not prepare yourself or set up properly for the next pair and suddenly you have lost two targets. Perhaps you let something going on around you become a distraction or some irrelevant thought enter your head, with the same result, poor concentration on the job in hand.

You may have shot four pairs perfectly on a stand and suddenly realise that you need just these last two for a perfect ten. Forget it. You'll come off with a nine or even an eight, unless you can completely clear your mind. This time the problem is that of becoming tense through trying too hard. Nothing works well if you tense up.

To shoot well in any situation you need to be physically relaxed yet mentally poised, ready to react in the right way when a target appears. This is easy to say, but difficult to do, and it is even more difficult to maintain that delicate balance needed to go on performing well. As you prepare to shoot, the one thing uppermost in your mind should be the next target, or pair of targets, though even with a pair of targets you must be prepared to give each in turn your full undivided attention.

'Enjoy!'

If on the other hand you have missed the previous target, you must try not to repeat the miss. If it is a shot you have successfully made many times before and the miss was caused by a concentration lapse, chastise yourself gently then forget about the lost target. Run the shot through in your mind, visualise the target breaking, take a deep breath, set yourself up correctly and pulverise the next one in the way you know you can.

If the missed target is one you have not dealt with before, then the solution is not so easy. Did you read it correctly? Should you have set up differently? Did you get any feed-back as you fired the shot? Did you realize as you pulled the trigger that you were behind, below, above, off line? Someone is bound to ask here, 'How do I know where my shot has gone?' Well, apart from the obvious signs of seeing your shot charge hit the ground or water (though even this can sometimes be quite 'misleading'), if, when you missed that previous target, you felt certain that your set-up and concentration were good you will often get an instinctive feel for where you missed it. This is something you should learn to believe in and profit from in

order to make a correction on the next target. If you have no instinctive feel for where you missed, this should also give a clue. Often what you are really saying by not being able to mark your shot is that you were not watching the target, so make up your mind when you call for the next one that whatever else happens you will build up and keep that all-important concentration on the target.

The most difficult misses to correct are the ones where you are convinced that everything was correct, that you had 'killed' it. In this situation you may well find yourself floundering and come away with a low score. Often the only solution here is to go off to a shooting ground, have a similar target set up and, perhaps with some helpful soul standing behind whispering in your ear, learn how to break it. Repeat the shot successfully a number of times so that you commit it to memory ready for the next time you come across it.

The one quality all top shooters seem to have in common is this tremendous ability to concentrate in a very single-minded way on the job in hand. It is even more than that; they seem able to switch this concentration on and off almost at will. One minute they may be laughing and joking with a group of friends but as soon as they prepare to shoot, their concentration is total. There is almost a personality change. Look at their eyes and you see a pretty mean machine, confident, often aggressively so; they've long overcome the fear of missing a target, nothing half-hearted here, total commitment to what they are doing. Job done, they will switch off again. They may make the whole thing look easy, but be assured that a great deal of hard work with many hours of practice has put them where they are.

Maybe their hearts do pound, their mouths go dry, their knees knock together like mine do when they step onto a competition stand, but you wouldn't know it—which is probably why I'm still coaching.

Remember: once you have established a reasonable gun fit, practise. Don't go looking for excuses in your stock shape. These days you can rarely blame a cartridge for a miss as they are manufactured to a high degree of consistency. The one big variable in the whole equation is YOU.

There is a great deal of information in this book, far too much to be absorbed in one reading, so hopefully you will go over each section several times and find something new each time you do so. I have tried to keep things fairly concise. One of the difficulties in attempting to write such a book is that everyone of you is different so that if I try to cover every variation, even on what might at first sight seem to be a very simple straightforward point, so many possibilities spring to mind that the whole thing is in danger of becoming one hugely tangled spider's web, rather like this sentence. For instance, if someone is taking a lesson and I pick out a mistake, I will try and relate what is happening as simply and as directly as possible so that more often than not within a few shots I will see some improvement made. Sometimes, however, no such improvement occurs so that I have a second go, perhaps re-wording or re-phrasing the point I am trying to make. Very often this second attempt is all it takes to put a point across, but sometimes I may say the same thing in four or five different ways, and still get no favourable response. In desperation I re-word things once more and it clicks, the light is switched on, usually accompanied by, 'Ah, now I know what you mean. Why didn't you say that before?' So if there is a point you do not understand, read it again, read around it, re-word it, listen for the click of the light-switch. Hopefully you will find at least some of it helpful.

If I have tempted anyone to get out and try a great sport, whether with clays or game, then it will all have been worthwhile—just don't blame me when it becomes obsessive.

As many of the friends and acquaintances I have made during numerous coaching trips 'across the pond' say, 'Enjoy!'

The stocks of the fifteen Sesquicentennial bar in wood hammer guns made in 1985 to commemorate the 150 years of Holland & Holland gun making from 1835 to 1985. Nine were built in 12-bore and six in 20-bore; all colour hardened finished with the hammers filed so that the gun could be opened in the cocking position. The guns were supplied in mahogany leather-lined French fitted wood cases in the style of the 1835 period.